KOREAN COOKING
FOR EVERYONE

Co-Published by Japan Publications Trading Co., Ltd and Joie, Inc.

Distributors:

UNITED STATES: Kodansha America, Inc., through Oxford University Press, 198 Madison Avenue, New York, NY 10016

CANADA: Fitzhenry & Whiteside Ltd., 195 Allstate Parkway, Markham, Ontario L3R 4T8

AUSTRALIA AND NEW ZEALAND: Bookwise International, 174 Cormack Road, Wingfield, SA 5013 Australia

ASIA AND OTHER COUNTRIES: Japan Publications Trading Co., Ltd., 1-2-1, Sarugaku-cho, Chiyoda-ku, Tokyo, 101-0064 Japan

Original Copyright ©2003 by Ji Sook Choe & Yukiko Moriyama

3rd Printing August 2006

World rights reserved Published by JOIE, INC. 1-8-3, Hirakawa-cho, Chiyoda-ku, Tokyo 102-0093 Japan

Printed in Japan

ISBN 13 : 978-4-88996-124-9

ISBN 10 : 4-88996-124-0

ACKNOWLEDGMENTS

Our grateful appreciation to the following individuals for their encouragement and patience throughout many months of complying the materials in this book:

Shiro Shimura, publisher of JOIE, INC.
Kyung Sik An, proprietor of KUSANOIE restaurant
Eiichi Takuma, photographer
Mariko Suzuki, illustrator
Akira Naito, chief editor
Mieko Nagasawa, editor
Fuki Kasugai, editorial assistance

Our most sincere thanks to Chef Wataru Ohashi for his collaboration and his generous gift of time and expertise.

INTRODUCTION

Korea is known as "The Land of the Morning Calm", and enjoys a rich cultural heritage recognized for 5000 years, and yet is generally less known to Westerners than are its neighbors, China and Japan. However, in recent years many people around the world have shown a decided interest in Korean culture and its cooking. Korean cuisine is a blend of old and modern tastes. Foods tend to be less oily than that of China, and not as bland as that of Japan; instead many are spicy and hot with red pepper. Perhaps the pungent relish KIM-CHEE, and BULKOGEE, barbecued meats, are best known to foreigners.

Since 100–200 BC Korea has cultivated white, short grain rice, has been the main staple of the populace. Grains and beans were produced in the south and millet in the north. The Korean peninsula, bounded on the west by the Yellow Sea and on the east by the Sea of Japan, has a long productive coastline rich in varieties of seafood. By the 3rd and 4th centuries AD, efficient agriculture and fishing techniques had developed and were the most important activities of everyday life. Meat was an accepted part of the diet since an earlier Mongol invasion. However with introduction of Buddhism during the 6th century, consumption was reduced. Between the 10th and 13th centuries, Korea was again under Mongol domination the preparation and consumption of meat widely and permanently established. Buddhism and its tenets diminished, along with the daily habit of tea drinking which has given way to today's soft drinks and alcoholic industries. By the end of the 14th century, Confucianism was the national religion and dominated Korean society.

Social and family stability were established, and royalty, nobility and the wealthy all enjoyed an increasingly affluent society. Special dishes such as Royal Hors d'Oeuvres (KU-JEOLPAN, See P78), and Royal Hot Pot (SINSEON–LO, See P96), were created then. During the 17th and 18th centuries hot red peppers, *kabocha* (Japanese pumpkin), tomatoes, corn, sweet potatoes, and peanuts were introduced to the south of the country, and potatoes to the north. The hot red peppers and sweet potatoes came from Japan, and since their introduction the hot red pepper has greatly influenced Korean cooking. Most noticeably KIMCHEE, Korea's most traditional dish. This pungent pickled cabbage preparation is seasoned with hot pepper, and each region has modified to it's own taste, from mild to very hot.

Food preservation techniques such as air drying and pickling were also developed during this period. A large variety of ingredients made it possible for people to create elaborate dishes when required, and to improve home-style cooking. The ethnic foods we are familiar with today have changed little since then. In olden days, the preparation of the daily meal was a time consuming task. Today, however, the modern kitchen with its convenient electric appliances has greatly simplified the cook's work. In recent years, Korean cooking has become very popular in Japan, and most of us seem to enjoy the spicy flavors. We have enjoyed the dishes while eating out, but are reluctant to try making them at home. Perhaps it is because we lack the knowledge and skills necessary, or feel hindered by the limited availability of ingredients. I, as a cooking teacher and an author of cook books, (*Tofu, Sushi,* Japanese), realized that it was time to introduce these delicious dishes not only to the Japanese people, but to Westerners as well.

So with this idea in mind I have often met with Mr. Kyung Sik An, a proprietor of Korean restaurants, Mrs. Ji Sook Choe and Chef Wataru Ohashi. They are experts on Korean cooking, and I have learned more about the cuisine from them. I would like to share my experiences with you. To make Korean dishes enjoyable for everyone, most of the recipes contained in this book have been adapted to Western taste, while others retain their authenticity. Emphasis has been placed on the preparation and cooking of quick and easy daily meals and most of the necessary ingredients are available either in large supermarkets or oriental grocery stores, with no special equipment needed.

What Mr. An, Mrs. Choe, Chef Ohashi, and I, have presented here is the very book that will, we feel, enable anyone to start from the beginning······

I hope this book will help you to enjoy the food as much as I have.

CONTENTS

ACKNOWLEDGEMENTS···3
INTRODUCTION··4
BASIC COOKING INFORMATION···8
MAP OF KOREA···9

Appetizers
ROLLED HAM   미나리말이 *(Minari Mari)* ·······································10
LEAF ROLLS   쌈—생채、숙채 *(Sam—Sengche, Sukche)* ·····················11
COUNTRY STYLE BEEF   장조림 *(Chang Jorim)* ·······························12
TOASTED *NORI* SEAWEED   김구이 *(Kim Kuee)* ······························13

Soups
OXTAIL SOUP   곰탕 *(Komtang)* ···14
◄VARIATION► COOKED RICE IN OXTAIL SOUP   국밥 *(Kukbap)* ···········15
VEGETABLE SOUP   우거지국 *(Woogoji Kuk)* ·································16
FISH SOUP   동태국 *(Tongtae Kuk)* ···17
CHICKEN SOUP   미역국 *(Miyeok Kuk)* ···18
COLD CUCUMBER SOUP   미역냉국 *(Miyeok Nengkuk)* ·······················19

Meats
BARBECUED MEAT   불고기 *(Bulkogee)* ··20
BAKED SPARERIBS   불갈비 *(Bulkalbee)* ··22
◄VARIATION►OVEN-BARBECUED SPARERIBS   갈비오븐구이 *(Kalbee Oven Kuee)*···23
SKEWERED BEEF AND VEGETABLES   꼬치구이 *(Kochi Kuee)* ·················24
SEASONED RAW BEEF   육회 *(Yukwe)* ···25
BEEF AND VEGETABLE HOT POT   소고기전골 *(Sokoki Chongol)* ············26
BRAISED SHORT RIBS WITH VEGETABLES   갈비찜 *(Kalbee Chim)* ···········28
STEAMED TONGUE   우설편육 *(Wousul Pyeonyuk)* ····························29
STIR-FRIED PORK WITH KIMCHEE   김치볶음 *(Kimchee Pokkum)* ············30
PORK AND KIMCHEE CASSEROLE   김치찌개 *(Kimchee Chighe)*···············31

Seafoods
FRESH FISH WITH HOT SAUCE   생선회 *(Sengseon Hwe)* ······················32
◄VARIATION► WHITE FISH SALAD   생선초고추장 무침 *(Sengseon Chokochujang Muchim)*···33
BOUILLABAISSE–KOREAN STYLE   해물전골 *(Haemul Chongol)* ···············34
HOT-SPICY FISH STEW   생선찌개 *(Sengseon Chighe)* ······················36
SPICY STIR-FRIED SQUID   오징어볶음 *(Ojingeo Pokkum)* ·················37
STEAMED FISH   도미찜 *(Tomi Chim)* ···38
BROILED FISH   조기구이 *(Chogi Kuee)* ··39
CLAM BAKE   조개찜 *(Choge Chim)* ···40
STEAMED CLAMS   대합찜 *(Taehap Chim)* ·······································41
CLAMS AND *WAKAME* SEAWEED   미역무침 *(Miyeok Muchim)* ···············42
SEAFOOD SALAD   해물사라다 *(Haemul Salad)* ································43

Vegetables
ASSORTED VEGETABLES   나물 *(Namool)* ··44
MIXED VEGETABLES WITH BEEF   잡채 *(Chapche)* ····························46
◄VARIATION► MIXED VEGETABLES WITH SEAFOOD   해물잡채 *(Haemul Chapche)*···47
SAUTÉED MUSHROOMS   버섯볶음 *(Beosot Pokkum)* ·························48
STIR-FRIED GARLIC STALKS   마늘종볶음 *(Maneulchong Pokkum)* ··········49
STIR-FRIED CUCUMBERS AND BEEF   오이볶음 *(Oee Pokkum)* ···············50
STEAMED SMALL GREEN PEPPERS   풋고추양념무침 *(Pootkochu Yangnyeom Muchim)* ···51
BOILED POTATOES AND BEEF   감자조림 *(Kamja Chorim)* ·····················52
DAIKON RADISH WITH CHICKEN   무조림 *(Moo Chorim)* ·····················53
STUFFED CABBAGE ROLLS   캬베츠말이 *(Cabbage Sam)* ······················54

Eggs

SEAFOOD AND VEGETABLE OMELET　전　*(Cheon)* ······················· 56
◀VARIATION▶KEBAB KOREAN STYLE　꼬치전　*(Kochi Cheon)* ··············· 57
ROLLED-EGG-OMELET　달걀말이　*(Talgyal Mari)* ······················· 58
STEAMED EGG CUSTARD　달걀찜　*(Talgyal Chim)* ······················· 59

Tofu

TOFU STEAK　두부스테이크　*(Tuboo Steak)* ······························· 60
BRAISED *TOFU*　두부조림　*(Tuboo Chorim)* ······························· 61
TOFU HOT POT　두부전골　*(Tuboo Cheongol)* ···························· 62
TOFU CASSEROLE WITH *MISO*　두부된장찌개　*(Toboo Toenjang Chighe)* ······ 63

Rice

VEGETABLES AND BEEF ON RICE　비빔밥　*(Bibimbap)* ····················· 64
COOKED RICE IN HOT BROTH　국밥　*(Kukbap)* ··························· 65
GRUEL RICE WITH VEGETABLES　야채죽　*(Yache Chook)* ················· 66
GRUEL RICE WITH CHICKEN　닭죽　*(Tak Chook)* ······················· 67
RICE WITH SOYBEAN SPROUTS　콩나물밥　*(Kongnamul Bap)* ············· 68
STIR-FRIED RICE　볶음밥　*(Bokkumbap)* ······························· 69
ROLLED RICE WITH *NORI* SEAWEED　김밥　*(Kimbap)* ····················· 70

Noodles

COLD NOODLE DISH　냉면　*(Nengmyeon)* ······························· 72
HOT NOODLE DISH　온면　*(Onmyeon)* ································· 74
COLD NOODLES WITH HOT SAUCE　비빔면　*(Bibimmyeon)* ················ 75
STEAMED BUNS　만두　*(Mandu)* ····································· 76
SHRIMP AND VEGETABLE WRAP-UPS　밀쌈　*(Milsam)* ···················· 78

Pickles

CHINESE CABBAGE KIMCHEE　배추김치　*(Pechu Kimchee)* ················· 80
DAIKON RADISH KIMCHEE　깍뚜기　*(Kaktookee)* ······················· 82
COLD KIMCHEE DRINKS　나박김치　*(Nabakkimchee)* ····················· 83
DAIKON RADISH PICKLES　무말랭이장아찌　*(Moomallengee Chang-a-chee)* ····· 84
GARLIC PICKLES　마늘장아찌　*(Maneul Chang-a-chee)* ··················· 85
SHISO LEAVES IN *MISO* PASTE　깻잎장아찌　*(Kennip Chang-a-chee)* ········· 86
HOT GREEN PEPPERS IN *MISO* PASTE　풋고추장아찌　*(Pootkochu Chang-a-chee)* ·················· 87

Preserves

SALTED OYSTERS·SALTED CLAMS　어리굴젓·조개젓　*(Orikul Cheot· Choge Cheot)* ·············· 88

INFORMATION

BASIC TIPS ··· 90
PREPARATION ··· 91
COOKING METHODS ··· 96
MENU PLANNING ·· 100
FACETS OF KOREAN CULTURE ··· 102
COOKING UTENSILS ·· 104
INGREDIENTS ·· 106
METRIC TABLES ·· 110
INDEX ·· 111

NOTE:
With each title a pronunciation guide is given. However the spelling may differ from the practical usage.

BASIC COOKING INFORMATION

★ 1 cup is equivalent to 240 ml in our recipes: (American cup measurement)
     1 American cup = 240 ml = 8 American fl oz
     1 British cup = 200 ml = 7 British fl oz
     1 Japanese cup = 200 ml

1 tablespoon = 15 ml   1 teaspoon = 5 ml

C=cup	T=tablespoon	t=teaspoon	fl=fluid	oz=ounce	lb=pound
ml=milliliter	g=gram	in=inch	cm=centimeter	F=Fahrenheit	C=Celsius

TABLES CONVERTING FROM U.S. CUSTOMARY SYSTEM TO METRICS

Liquid Measures

U.S. Customary system	oz	g	ml
1/16 cup = 1 T	1/2 oz	14 g	15 ml
1/4 cup = 4 T	2 oz	60 g	59 ml
1/2 cup = 8 T	4 oz	115 g	118 ml
1 cup = 16 T	8 oz	225 g	236 ml
1 3/4 cups	14 oz	400 g	414 ml
2 cups = 1 pint	16 oz	450 g	473 ml
3 cups	24 oz	685 g	710 ml
4 cups	32 oz	900 g	946 ml

Liquid Measures

Japanese system	oz	ml
1/8 cup	7/8 oz	25 ml
1/4 cup	1 3/4 oz	50 ml
1/2 cup	3 1/2 oz	100 ml
1 cup	7 oz	200 ml
1 1/2 cups	10 1/2 oz	300 ml
2 cups	14 oz	400 ml
3 cups	21 oz	600 ml
4 cups	28 oz	800 ml

Weights

ounces to grams*
1/4 oz = 7 g
1/2 oz = 14 g
1 oz = 30 g
2 oz = 60 g
4 oz = 115 g
6 oz = 170 g
8 oz = 225 g
16 oz = 450 g

*Equivalent

Linear Measures

inches to centimeters
1/2 in = 1.27 cm
1 in = 2.54 cm
2 in = 5.08 cm
4 in = 10.16 cm
5 in = 12.7 cm
10 in = 25.4 cm
15 in = 38.1 cm
20 in = 50.8 cm

Temperatures

Fahrenheit (F) to Celsius (C)	
freezer storage	−10°F = −23.3°C
	0°F = −17.7°C
water freezes	32°F = 0 °C
	68°F = 20 °C
	100°F = 37.7°C
water boils	212°F = 100 °C
	300°F = 148.8°C
	400°F = 204.4°C

Deep-Frying Oil Temperatures

300°F − 330°F (150°C − 165°C) = low
340°F − 350°F (170°C − 175°C) = moderate
350°F − 360°F (175°C − 180°C) = high

MAP OF KOREA

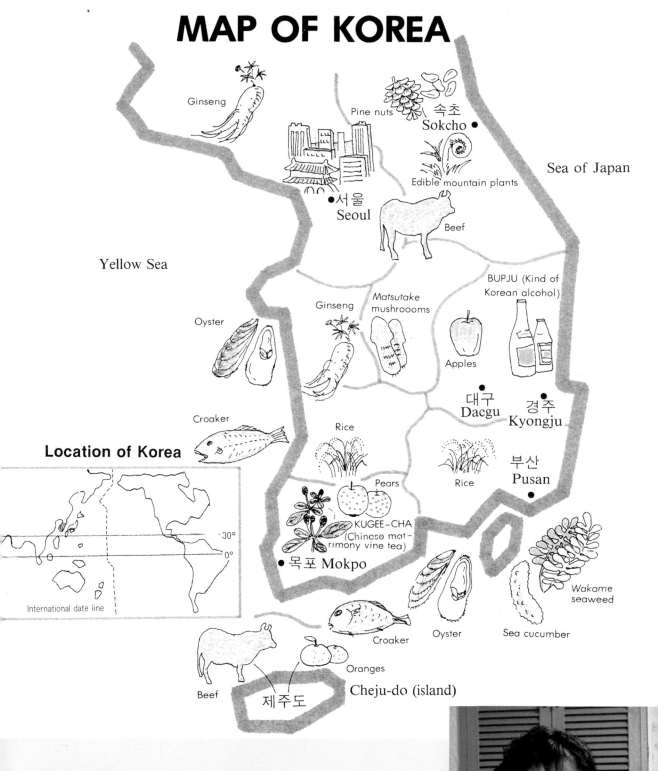

Ginseng

Pine nuts

속초
Sokcho ●

Sea of Japan

Edible mountain plants

서울
Seoul

Beef

Yellow Sea

BUPJU (Kind of
Korean alcohol)

Oyster

Ginseng

Matsutake
mushrooms

Apples

대구
Dacgu

경주
Kyongju

Croaker

Location of Korea

Rice

Pears

Rice

부산
Pusan

30°

0°

KUGEE–CHA
(Chinese mat-
rimony vine tea)

목포 Mokpo

Wakame
seaweed

International date line

Croaker

Oyster

Sea cucumber

Oranges

Beef

제주도

Cheju-do (island)

About author   **JI SOOK CHOE**

Ji Sook Choe was born in Seoul, 1941. Having studied aesthetics
at Seoul University, she was actively engaged in theater and televi-
sion as a popular actress—announcer.
She came to Japan to study classical theaters and now studies *Noh*
under kimpo Hamano of *Kanze* school. As well as "harvesting"
Japanese culture, Ji Sook Choe contributes in "raising" the quality of Korean Cookery in Japan. She is an advisor to "KUSANOIE",
a Korean restaurant in Akasaka, Tokyo.

This elegant and colorful cold dish can be served at any banquet table.

20 slices parma ham (10½ oz, 300 g)
20 stalks Japanese parsley or green
   onion
20 pine nuts
Salt
Dip
{ 1 T vinegar
{ 2 T soy sauce

* Subtitute parma ham with thinly sliced honey roast ham.
  Japanese parsley is prized for its fragrance and crispness. Cook in salted boiling water and rinse well under running water to remove the harshness. It is rich in calcium, vitamin A and C. If not available, substitute with green onion.
* Adjust the taste of dip by adding crushed pine nuts or fresh ginger juice. Lemon juice also gives good accent.
* Pine nuts are a must in Korean cookery. They accompany alcohol, and are used as a garnish in many dishes.

1. Wash Japanese parsley thoroughly and cut off roots at white part. Heat salted water to boiling point. Add Japanese parsley root ends first.

2. Blanch well in cold water and drain.

3. Roll each slice of ham, towards far end.

4. Take one stalk of Japanese parsley. Place rolled ham onto the root end and roll up together tightly. Arrange on plate, rolled ends down. Top each with a pine nut. Mix dip ingredients and place in center.

Making your own rolls is particularly fun at an intimate party.

INGREDIENTS: 4–6 servings

½ bunch red leaf lettuce (bronze lettuce)
½ head cabbage
SAM JANG (light flavored *miso*)

A {
3 hot green peppers or small green peppers
2 green peppers
4 in (10cm) green onion
⅓ oz (10g) garlic

B {
½ cup KOCHU JANG (hot sauce— See P95)
1 cup red *miso*
1½ cups white *miso*
{
2 T sesame oil
1 T sake

C {
2 oz (60g) sugar
1 T ground sesame seeds
2 t soy sauce
½ t MSG
Ground chili pepper
Pepper

Cooked rice (See P92)
Vegetable sticks

* Make double quantity of SAM JANG and keep in refrigerator for later use.
* Roll barbecued meat or KIMCHEE with red leaf lettuce like eating tacos. This is a popular party offering.

1. Chop first three of **A** ingredients finely. Peel garlic and crush.

2. In a bowl, combine all **B** ingredients.

3. Add (1) and all **C** ingredients. Blend well.

4. Blanch red leaf lettuce in cold water to add crispness. Cook cabbage leaves briefly in boiling water. Drain leaves and pat dry. Spread a leaf, put a small amount of rice and (3) sauce. Dip vegetable sticks into sauce.

Prepare in advance and serve as a cold appetizer or as a side dish.

INGREDIENTS: 4–6 servings

1 lb (450g) beef shank

A
{
7 cups water
4 T soy sauce
3⅓ T *sake* or wine
2 T *mirin*
¼ t sugar
5 cloves garlic
1 oz (30g) fresh ginger root
5–6 black peppercorns
}

3 eggs
6 small green peppers

* Use eggs which are at room temperature. Cook in plenty of boiling water with a pinch of salt. Bring to a boil and carefully lower the heat. Simmer for 10 minutes for hard boiled eggs, 5 minutes for soft boiled eggs.
* The "hidden" flavor is caught out of the beef shank when it is simmered slowly. This is an economical dish. If you want to save time also, cut the meat into pieces before cooking.
* Serve chilled the next day as an appetizer. It keeps well in refrigerator.

1. In saucepan, add beef and **A** ingredients. Bring to a boil on high heat. Remove residue and reduce heat.

2. Cover and simmer for 2–3 hours until tender, turning over the meat occasionally to give flavor evenly.

3. Cook hard boiled eggs and shell. Add to the pan and cook until they "wear" the brown color (approx 20 minutes).

4. Remove stems of small green peppers and add to the pan. Cook just until tender. Cut meat into ¼ in (0.7cm) slices, eggs into wedges. Arrange on serving plate.

Crispy seaweed and sesame seeds are a wonderful combination.

INGREDIENTS: 4 servings

4 sheets roasted *nori* seaweed
4 t sesame oil
1/2 t roasted sesame seeds
Salt
MSG

＊ Roasted *nori* seaweed is eaten as a topping for cooked rice. The aroma of roasted sesame seeds as well as *nori* seaweed stimulates the appetite. Roast just before serving since it soon loses the flavor.
＊ If too many sesame seeds come off when roasted, use ground seeds.
＊ Shake salt and MSG from high position for even seasoning.

1. On one side of *nori* seaweed, brush on sesame oil evenly. Sprinkle with salt and MSG lightly.

2. Sprinkle with sesame seeds evenly.

3. Carefully roast both sides. Do not burn.

4. Cut each sheet into 8 ths.

OXTAIL SOUP 곰탕 *(Komtang)*

Slow simmering of oxtail brings out an irresistible rich homemade flavor.

INGREDIENTS: 4 servings

2 lbs (900g) oxtail
Salt and pepper
MSG
Finely chopped green onion
　for garnish

* This recipe can be used for any joint of meat, making a rich flavored opaque soup.
* Season very lightly and let everyone adjust the taste at the table with soy sauce mixed with crushed garlic, ground chili pepper, and grated ginger root, or simply with salt and pepper.
* When meat is tender, remove from heat and let stand for one night. Remove the floating fat.

1. In a saucepan, add oxtail and enough water to cover. Bring to a boil and discard water. Rinse oxtail to remove any scum.

2. Bring 1 gal (3.5–4 lit) of water to a boil. Add oxtail. Remove residue thoroughly, then reduce to medium heat. Cover and simmer 3–4 hours, keeping the meat covered with water.

3. Insert a skewer and if the meat can be easily removed from the bone, it is tender enough. Adjust the seasoning. Sprinkle with finely chopped green onion and serve.

OXTAILS

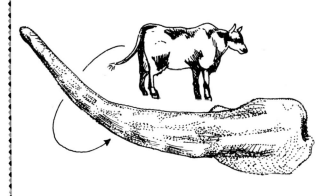

Oxtails make excellent soups or stews when cooked in liquid for a long time. Oxtails are usually sold ready-to-cook when purchasing such oxtail, choose larger rounds since they are meatier and more flavorful than small ones.
If using whole oxtails, prepare as directed below. In any case, long and slow cooking is essential.

[Preparation]
Remove the fat and membrane around the thicker part. The tip has less fat, but remove membrane. Run a finger along the tail to find indented joints.

◄ VARIATION ► **COOKED RICE IN OXTAIL SOUP** 국밥 (*Kukbap*)

This recipe makes an ideal one-bowl dish for people who have over indulged or are out of sort.

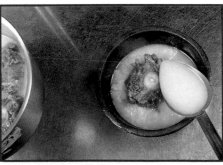

In serving bowl, put hot cooked rice. Pour over **oxtail soup** and sprinkle with finely chopped green onion. Serve with KIMCHEE, salt and pepper.

15

2 oz (60g) dried *daikon* radish leaves
2 hot green peppers
1/2 green onion
3 1/2 cup *dashi* stock (See P94)
2 oz (60g) red *miso*
2 oz (60g) white *miso*
1/2 t crushed garlic
Sesame oil

∗ This soup is originally made of the outer leaves of Chinese cabbage or *daikon* radish leaves which are apt to be thrown away. If you have no such leaves, cook with any green leaves.
∗ It is recommended that whenever you purchase *daikon*, dry the leaves in the shade and store.

Any dried vegetable can be used in this soup.

1. Soak *daikon* leaves in water overnight.

2. Drain and squeeze out water lightly. Cut into 2 in (5cm) length and boil lightly.

3. Chop hot green peppers. Slice green onion diagonally.

4. In a saucepan heat stock to boiling. Add *daikon* radish leaves and cook over medium heat 3–4 minutes.

5. Dissolve *miso* into liquid, add garlic and bring to a boil.

6. Stir in hot green peppers and green onion, then remove from heat immediately. Sprinkle a few drops of sesame oil just before serving, if desired.

Steaming bowl of easy-to-make fish soup is very nourishing.

INGREDIENTS: 4 servings

14 oz (400 g) cod fillets
7 oz (200 g) *daikon* radish
2 green onions
5–6 stalks chrysanthemum leaves or
   watercress
1/4 t crushed garlic

A { 1 1/2 t salt
   1/2 t sake
   1/4 t soy sauce
   Pepper

Sesame oil

＊If using salted cod, test for saltness before seasoning.
＊If chrysanthemum leaves are not available, substitute with watercress.

1. Peel *daikon* and cut into quarter rounds. In a saucepan, heat sesame oil and add *daikon* and crushed garlic. Cook and stir 3–4 minutes.

2. Add 4 cups water and cook until *daikon* is tender. Cut cod into bite size pieces and add to the pan. Heat just to boiling.

3. Cut green onion into 2 in (5 cm) and stir in, season with **A**. Tear chrysanthemum leaves and add to the soup; remove from heat. Sprinkle with ground chili pepper, if desired.

This soup will add a new dimension to your favorite repertoire.

INGREDIENTS: 4 servings

7 oz (200g) boneless chicken thigh or
   10½ oz (300g) chicken thigh
⅓ oz (10g) dried *wakame* seaweed
4 cups beef stock (See P94)
A { 2 t salt
    Crushed garlic
    MSG
½ t soy sauce
Finely chopped green onion for garnish
Shredded omelet (See P94)

* This soup is a regular attendant to birthday parties. Koreans also encourage pregnant women to consume as much *wakame* soup as possible since *wakame* soup provides them with calcium and iron which they generally lack in pregnancy.

* Soak *wakame* seaweed in water 10 minutes. Note that it multiplies its volume 10 times. A good quality *wakame* seaweed has thinner stems and shiny leaves when soaked.

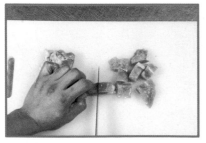

1. Cut chicken into bite size pieces. Cut soaked *wakame* seaweed into 1 in (2.5 cm) length.

2. Heat beef stock and chicken to a boil. Stir in **A** ingredients, constantly skimming residue.

3. Stir in soy sauce, then remove from heat. Add *wakame* seaweed. Pour into each serving bowl and sprinkle with finely chopped green onion and shredded omelet.

An ideal refreshing summer time soup.

⅓ oz (10g) dried *wakame* seaweed
2 small cucumbers
1 white part of green onion
5 cups water
2 chicken bouillon cubes

A ⎰ 1 T soy sauce
⎱ 1 t vinegar
⎱ 1 t roasted sesame seeds
⎱ Salt and pepper

Sesame oil
Ground chili pepper
Dash of salt

∗ Boil water and cool for a better taste. It is worth the trouble. Use mineral water if available.
∗ Chill serving bowls beforehand. Float ice cubes to please the eye.

1. Cut off ends of cucumbers. Slice thinly and sprinkle with salt; set aside. Cut *wakame* seaweed into 1 in (2.5cm) length. Cut green onion into 1½ in (4cm) and shred. Blanch in cold water to remove harshness.

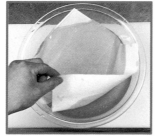

2. Heat water and bouillon cubes to boiling; let stand to cool. Spread paper towel on surface and remove excess fat.

3. Add *wakame* seaweed. Lightly rinse cucumbers and stir in.

4. Stir in **A** ingredients. Just before serving, sprinkle with shredded green onion, sesame oil and chili pepper.

BARBECUED MEAT 불고기 (Bulkogee)

One of the best known and the most popular Korean dishes.

$^1\!/_2$ lb (225g) beef rib steak
$^1\!/_2$ lb (225g) boneless chicken thigh
$^1\!/_2$ lb (225g) pork loin
$^1\!/_2$ lb (225g) mutton or lamb steak
Marinade
$\begin{cases} ^1\!/_2 \text{ cup } \textbf{Barbecue Sauce A} \\ ^1\!/_2 \text{ cup } \textbf{Barbecue Sauce B} \end{cases}$
Roasted sesame seeds
Finely chopped green onion
Vegetables to your taste (onion, green pepper, green onion, eggplant or pumpkin slices)

* **Barbecue hints:** Preheat grill well, then put meats on. Turn when one side is done. Never turn again since the meat loses its flavorful juice and becomes too crusty.
* It is recommended to grill vegetables for nutritive balance and a change. Cut green peppers lengthwise into halves or quarters. Slice green onion diagonally. Cut pumpkin, garlic or carrot into $^1\!/_8$ in (0.3cm) slices for easy cooking.
* Red leaf lettuce (bronze lettuce) can also be rolled with other accompaniments (See P 11).

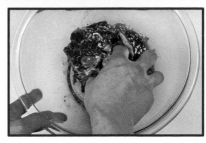

1. Prepare Barbecue Sauce A. Mix roasted sesame seeds and finely chopped green onion, if desired. Cut beef and chicken into bite size pieces (1/8 in, 0.3 cm thick).

2. Prepare Barbecue Sauce B. Slice pork and mutton.

3. Rub sauce A into beef and chicken with finger tips. Rub sauce B into pork and mutton with finger tips. Preheat grill and cook meats. Do not overcook. Serve with Barbecue Sauces A and B.

Barbecue Sauces

A: soy sauce base

INGREDIENTS: Makes 4 cups

1/2 medium apple, quartered and sliced
1 oz (30 g) ginger root, thinly sliced
1 oz (30 g) garlic, thinly sliced
2 cups soy sauce
1/2 cup each sake and mirin
1/4 cup water
6 oz (170 g) sugar
1/2 t MSG

* This plain and mild sauce goes well with simple tasting meats such as beef or chicken.
* Marinate meats no longer than 20 minutes, or they lose tenderness.

1. Combine all ingredients and cook over high heat. Bring to a boil and reduce heat. Cook 15 minutes. Reduce heat again and simmer a further 15 minutes; let stand to cool overnight.

2. When ready to use, strain the mixture and add roasted sesame seeds and chopped green onion.

B: *miso* base

INGREDIENTS: Makes 4 cups

4 oz (115 g) each red and white *miso*
2 oz (60 g) KOCHU JANG (hot sauce – See P 95)
1 oz (30 g) garlic, crushed
1 oz (30 g) green onion, chopped finely
1/4 cup sesame oil
1 T ground chili pepper
1 T roasted sesame seeds
1 t ginger juice
Pepper
2 1/4 cups **Barbecue Sauce A** (See above)

* A hot and rich flavored sauce. Goes well with rich tasting meats such as mutton or lamb.

1. Combine red and white *miso*, KOCHU JANG (hot sauce), sugar, crushed garlic, finely chopped green onion, ground chili pepper, ginger juice and pepper. Blend well with fingers.

2. Add remaining ingredients and mix well.

Commercial Barbecue Sauces

If you are busy and trying to stretch your time, use commercial barbecue sauces as a base. Blend with *miso*, finely chopped green onion or any spices and seasonings of your choice. It makes a great difference.

BAKED SPARERIBS 불갈비 *(Bulkalbee)*

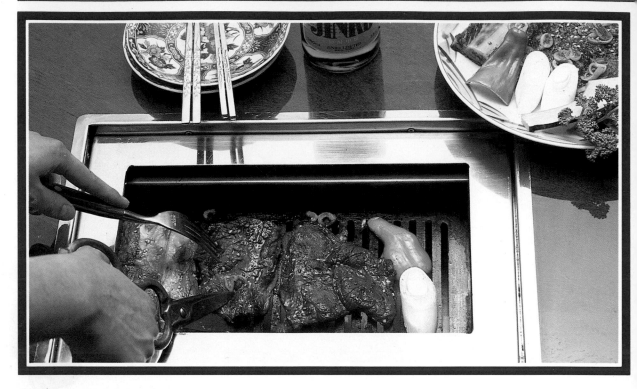

A special marinade transforms the ribs into a mouthwatering delicacy.

4 beef sparerib pieces
Marinade Sauce
2 cups **Barbecue Sauce A**
(See P21)

* Beef and pork spareribs are valued as the highest quality meat in Korea.
* Cut grilled spareribs into bite size pieces using cooking scissors.

1. Cut spareribs into serving pieces.

2. Remove film covering the meat carefully.

3. Remove excess fat and membrane from the bone side.

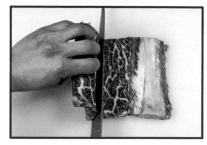

4. With meaty side down, insert knife just under bone and slice as shown, leaving the end uncut. Open out flat.

5. Then slice the meat into half thickness, leaving the end uncut and open out flat.

6. Make a slit along the center of each bone. This eases the membrane when grilled and makes the meat apart easily.

7. In a large bowl place spareribs and pour over marinade. Rub and turn with fingers; let stand 15 minutes. Bake both sides on preheated grill.

BEEF CUTS YOU SHOULD KNOW

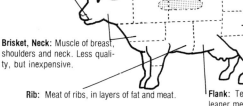

Chuck: Shoulder meat including most of neck, parts about the shoulder blade, and those about the first three ribs.

Tongue: An elastic texture when grilled is prized, as well as cooked in stew.

Brisket, Neck: Muscle of breast, shoulders and neck. Less quality, but inexpensive.

Rib: Meat of ribs, in layers of fat and meat.

Loin Roasts: Thick and wide meat on back ribs. Fatty loin makes a good Korean barbecue.

Filet Mignón: Round and narrow meat along inside of backbone. The best quality beef for its tenderness and leanness.

Rump: Rather firm meat on top of hip, between loin and round.

Oxtail: Skinned tail, good for soup.

Round: Lean meat of thigh, between rump and leg, cooked in various ways. The part between round and loin is called sirloin Tip and is good for tartar steak.

Shank: Toughest . meat from lower part of leg, good for stew.

Flank: Tender part of round, between ribs and hip. This leaner meat should not be overcooked.

◀ VARIATION ▶ OVEN-BARBECUED SPARERIBS 갈비오븐구이 *(Kalbee Oven Kuee)*

Cook the marinated spareribs in the oven.

Preheat oven to 425°F (220°C). Place spareribs on a wire rack. Cook until done turning and brushing with the marinade sauce occasionally. Serve on red leaf lettuce (bronze lettuce) and lemon wedges.

These tempting beef and vegetables are carefully arranged.

INGREDIENTS: 4 servings (8 skewers)

For 7–8 in (18–20cm) skewers:
¼ lb (115g) boneless beef steak
¼ lb (115g) beef liver
½ medium squid
4 shrimp
4 pickling onions
2 green peppers
1 medium tomato
Sauce
{ ¼ cup **Barbecue Sauce A**
    (See P21)
{ 1T roasted sesame seeds

* Wash beef liver in water, pressing out blood. Skin. Fresh liver has no odor and is highly nutritious.
* For preparing squid, see P 34, P 35 and P 37.
* If using regular onion, cut into wedges leaving the core uncut.

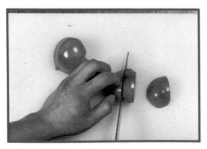

1. Cut tomato into 6 or 8 wedges.

2. Cut beef, liver into bite size pieces. Remove entrails and legs from squid, peel and cut into diamond pattern, cut into 1 in (2.5cm) width. Rinse shrimp in salted water. Cut green peppers in half.

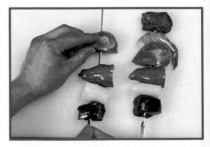

3. Skewer ingredients colorfully onto 8 metal skewers. Cook on barbecue grill, griddle or barbecue plate, occasionally brushing with sauce.

This delicately seasoned beef dish is traditionally served with raw egg yolk.

INGREDIENTS: Per serving

¼ lb (115g) beef for tartar steak
1 small cucumber

A ⎰ 2T **Barbecue Sauce A** (See P21)
   ½ t sesame oil
   ½ t roasted sesame seeds
  ⎱ Crushed garlic

1 egg yolk
½ t pine nuts
½ pear

* If pears are available, serve as a garnish. Cut into fine julienne strips and place on sliced cucumber. Then top with the meat. It is said that pears prevent food poisoning when eaten with raw meat.

* Use lean beef such as round steak or sirloin tip. Make sure that it is absolutely fresh.

* This dish, known as "YUKWE", is very similar to tartar steak in Europe, and no wonder. Tartar was brought to Europe by the Tatars, a horse-riding people of Mongolia who are supposed to have introduced this special dish to Korea.

1. Cut off ends of cucumber. Cut in half then into thin slices. On serving plate, arrange in all directions.

2. Slice beef into ⅛ in (0.3 cm) thickness, then into shreds working parallel to fibers.

3. Toss shredded meat with **A.**

4. Make a small heap of meat in center of the plate. Make a "well" on top and pour in egg yolk. Crush and chop pine nuts, sprinkle over yolk. Mix all when eating.

This colorful casserole is elegant enough to be served at any banquet table.

INGREDIENTS: 4 servings

¾ lb (340g) boneless lean beef

A
- 2½ T soy sauce
- 1½ T each *sake* and *mirin*
- 1 t sugar
- ¼ t sesame oil
- ¼ t roasted sesame seeds
- ⅛ t crushed garlic
- ⅛ t *dashi-no-moto* (instant stock– See P94)
- ⅓ oz (10g) green onion, chopped finely
- Pepper and MSG

2 Chinese cabbage leaves (5 oz, 140g)
½ (1½ oz, 45g) medium carrot

2 dried *shiitake* mushrooms, soaked in water.
½ bunch green onion

Soup Stock
- 3½ cups beef stock (See P94)
- 3 t each salt and soy sauce
- 2 t each sugar and *mirin*
- 1 t sesame oil
- ⅔ oz (20g) green onion, chopped finely

1 egg

* This dish is one of the two serving styles of Korean hot pots. For details, see P 96.

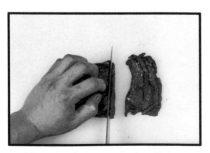

1. Slice beef into ⅛ in (0.3cm) thickness.

2. Then cut into strips.

3. In a bowl, combine beef and ingredients **A**, rubbing with fingers.

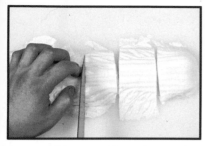

4. Cut Chinese cabbage into 2 in (5cm) length.

5. Then into strips cutting lengthwise.

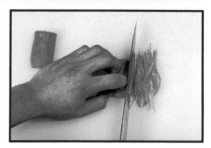

6. Cut carrot into 2 in (5cm) long strips.

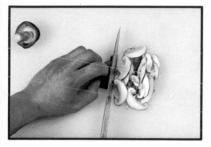

7. Remove stems of mushrooms; cut into strips.

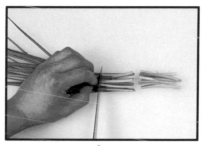

8. Cut green onion into 2 in (5cm) length.

9. Showing prepared ingredients.

10. In a 8 in (20cm) shallow pan, add ¾ quantity of Chinese cabbage. Flatten the surface.

11. Divide meat mixture into 6. Place ⅙ in center, making a "well" on top. Place remaining portions in all directions.

12. Place green onion as shown.

13. Arrange carrot, mushrooms and remaining quarter of Chinese cabbage neatly.

14. In another saucepan combine ingredients for soup stock and bring to a boil. Heat (13) pan and pour over soup.

15. Drop egg yolk into the "well". Cook until heated through, and help yourself mixing meat, egg yolk and vegetables. Add more stock if necessary.

1³/₄ lbs (800g) beef spareribs
Marinade Sauce
- 5 T soy sauce
- 2¹/₂ T each *sake* and *mirin*
- 3¹/₂ t sugar
- ¹/₂ t crushed garlic
- ¹/₈ t ground chili pepper
- Pepper

¹/₃ medium carrot (1¹/₂ oz, 50g)
2 dried *shiitake* mushrooms, soaked
  in water
1 green onion
1 green pepper
2¹/₂ oz (70g) bamboo shoot (canned)
1 T each salad oil and *mirin*
1 t roasted sesame seeds
Shredded omelet (See P94)

＊For richer flavor, add boiled chestnuts, ginkgo nuts or pine nuts if available.

Slow cooking makes the meat tender, and sesame seeds and red chili pepper enrich the taste.

1. Cut spareribs into serving pieces. Remove any membrane and excess fat (See P 22). Place bone side down, and make a deep slit in center. Then using the knife flat, slice meat in half leaving the end uncut. Slice the other side and open out flat.

2. Make incisions at ¹/₄ in (0.7cm) intervals. This process not only helps the meat to absorb the marinade but also makes eating easier.

3. Combine all marinade ingredients and add spareribs. Let stand 3–4 hours.

4. In a saucepan, heat 1 T salad oil. Add drained spareribs and cook over high heat. Reserve the marinade sauce.

5. Pour enough water to cover and simmer until the meat is tender. Add remaining marinade and continue to cook, until the liquid is boiled down to half, constantly skimming.

6. Slice carrot. Cut up remaining vegetables and add to the pan. When heated through, stir in *mirin* to glaze. Pour in sesame oil and immediately remove from heat. Sprinkle with sesame seeds and shredded omelet.

Miso, **soy bean paste, makes a superlative tongue dish.**

INGREDIENTS: 4 servings

1 whole beef tongue (2¼ lbs, 1 kg)

A ⎧ 1 green part of green onion
⎪ ⅔ oz (20g) ginger root, thinly sliced
⎨ ⅔ oz (20g) garlic, thinly sliced
⎪ 1 T *sake* or white wine
⎪ 1 t salt
⎩ ½ t peppercorns

4 oz (100g) each red and white *miso*

Garnishes
Pickling onions, celery, chrysanthemum leaves, parsley, etc.

* A small beef tongue weighs 2¼ lbs (1 kg). Peel off the rough black skin. It is cooked slowly with herbs and vegetables and spices until a skewer is inserted easily.
* Slice just before serving. The surface of the tongue can lose its moisture and color easily, therefore its flavor too.

1. Peel off skin of tongue. Put in a pan and cover with enough water to cover (approx 2 gal, 8 lit). Add ingredients **A** and cook over high heat.

2. Bring to a boil, then reduce heat. Simmer 1 hour and half uncovered, constantly removing residue. When the meat is done, remove from heat and let stand to cool.

3. Drain and dry with paper towel. Mix same amount of red and white *miso* and coat the tongue. Keep in airtight container and chill overnight. Just before serving, remove *miso* and lightly rince in water. Pat-dry and slice into ⅛ in (0.3cm). Garnish with herbal vegetables. Serve with vinegar and soy sauce.

An ordinary pork dish is colorfully and tastily transformed with spicy-sour KIMCHEE.

INGREDIENTS: 4 servings

½ lb (225g) boned pork rib
14 oz (400g) **CHINESE CABBAGE KIM-CHEE** (See P80)
4 green onions
2 T salad oil
Salt and pepper

A
{
1 t crushed garlic
½ t ground chili pepper
½ t *dashi-no-moto* (instant stock —See P94)
}

½ t roasted sesame seeds

* It is preferable to use a little old KIM-CHEE which is getting sour, to cook with fatty rib. There is a reason. The pork fat melts when cooked, and has a natural affinity for organic acid such as lactic or acetic acid. This means that fat and acid get along very well. As a result, a good harmony is achieved when pork and hot sour KIMCHEE are combined with each other.
* If the rib is too fatty, preboil to remove excess fat.

1. Cut pork rib into ³/₁₆ in (0.5cm) thickness, KIMCHEE into 1½ in (4cm), and green onion into 2 in (5cm) length.

2. In a saucepan heat salad oil and add pork. Cook and stir over high heat. Season with salt and pepper.

3. Stir in KIMCHEE. Add green onion and ingredients **A** and stir-fry briefly. Place in serving bowl, sprinkle with roasted sesame seeds.

INGREDIENTS: 4 servings

½ lb (225g) boneless pork chop
14 oz (400g) **CHINESE CABBAGE KIMCHEE** (See P80)
3 cups beef stock (See P94)

A
- ½ t *dashi-no-moto* (instant stock–See P94)
- ¼ t crushed garlic
- Salt
- Ground chili pepper

12 oz (340g) *tofu*
4 dried *shiitake* mushrooms, soaked in water
2 green onions
¼ bunch chrysanthemum leaves or watercress
3 T salad oil

∗ If using frozen meat, slice before completely thawed.

Pork goes well with hot-spicy vegetable pickles.

1. Slice pork into ³⁄₁₆ in (0.5cm). Cut KIMCHEE into ⅛ in (0.3cm) length.

2. In a pan over medium heat, in hot oil, cook and stir pork.

3. When meat is nearly done, stir in drained KIMCHEE. Reserve the KIMCHEE liquid.

4. Stir in the liquid and continue to cook. Add beef stock, bring to a boil; remove from heat.

5. In a shallow saucepan, arrange cut-up *tofu*, *shiitake* mushrooms (make a decorative crisscross on top), and slivered green onion.

6. Add (4) and heat. When *tofu* begins to shake, add chrysanthemum leaves, tough stems removed.

31

FRESH FISH WITH HOT SAUCE 생선회 *(Sengseon Hwe)*

" 회 (Hwe)" is a word used to describe food without any cooking or food blanched for a few seconds. This special dipping sauce excites the taste buds.

INGREDIENTS: 4 servings

9–10 oz (250–285g) fresh white meat fish fillets (sea bream, sole, etc)
1 small cucumber
1 small carrot
1/4 medium *daikon* radish or celery
Dip
- 1³/4 oz (50g) KOCHU JANG (hot sauce – See P 95)
- 1¹/3 T sugar
- 1 T sesame oil
- 1 T vinegar
- 1¹/2 t soy sauce
- 1 t roasted sesame seeds

- ²/3 t crushed garlic
- MSG
- Ground chili pepper
1 T pine nuts

* The Koreans eat fish au naturel with a special dip made of KOCHU JANG (hot sauce – See P 95). They enjoy fish of great variety with this sauce.

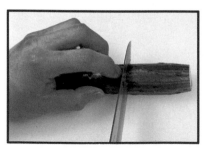

1. Cut off end of cucumber and cut into 2 in (5cm).

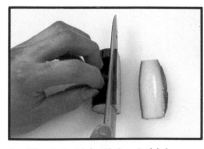

2. Slice into 1/8 in (0.3cm) thickness.

3. Finely cut into julienne strips.

4. Cut carrot and *daikon* radish alike.

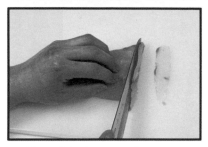

5. Slice fish into ⅛ in (0.3cm) thickness.

6. On a serving plate, lay vegetables in all directions.

7. Now the bed of vegetables is ready.

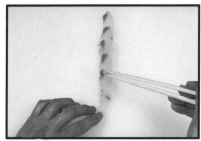

8. On chopping board arrange fish slices in overlapping layers.

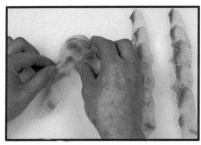

9. Curl anticlockwise to shape the center of the flower, darker side up.

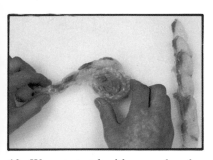

10. Wrap around with second and, third layers, finally shaping into a flower.

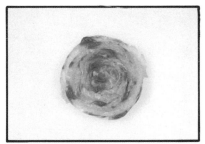

11. Place in center of vegetable bed. Using side of knife sprinkle the "flower" with crushed pine nuts. Combine dip ingredients and serve in a small bowl.

◀ VARIATION ▶ **WHITE FISH SALAD** 생선초고추장무침 *(Sengseon Chokochujang Muchim)*

1. In a bowl combine fish slices, *daikon* radish, cucumber, carrot slices and chopped pine nuts.

2. Combine dip ingredients. Add to (1) and toss well.

A rich variety of shellfish and fish are cooked in a broth.

INGREDIENTS: 4 servings

1 (1 lb, 450g) sea bream or croaker
1 fillet (7 oz, 200g) cod
1 (10 oz, 285g) squid
1 medium crab
4 shrimp, deveined
4 miniature octopus
4 oz (115g) oysters
4 each clams and mussels in shell
4 boiled scallops
8 short neck clams in shell
3½ oz (100g) *daikon* radish
⅓ bunch Japanese parsley or green onion

4 oz (115g) *tofu*
5½ cups *dashi* stock (See P94)

A $\begin{cases} 1\frac{3}{4} \text{ oz (50g) KOCHU JANG (hot sauce–See P95)} \\ 1\frac{1}{3} \text{ T } sake \\ 1 \text{ t salt} \\ \frac{1}{2} \text{ t crushed garlic} \end{cases}$

∗ A copper pan used for bouillabaisse is ideal.
∗ Choose any fish or shellfish to your taste.

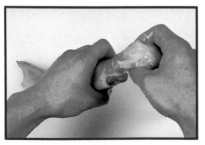

1. Insert a finger into body of squid and separate the joint. Gently pull out tentacles and entrails.

2. Tentacles and entrails are pulled out. Be careful not to break the sac.

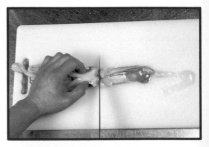

3. Cut off entrails.

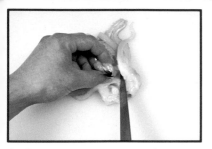

4. Cut to open out tentacles. Remove eyeballs and beak ball.

5. Cut body and tentacles into bite size.

6. Discard the triangular shell at the bottom of crab.

7. Insert thumb into the space just made, open up the shell.

8. Using the knife tip, remove the spongy finger-like gills.

9. Cut into halves, then into pieces.

10. Make incision into the base of leg.

11. Work into the claw as well.

12. Remove scales and entrails from fish and cut into bite size, with bone attached. Soak clams in salted water to remove sand in advance. Rinse oysters briefly in salted water.

13. In a saucepan add *dashi* stock and **A** seasonings, bring to a boil. Add crab and fish, bring to another boil. Add *daikon* radish sliced in half-moons.

14. When *daikon* radish is heated through, add all seafood except oysters. When clams open up, remove from heat.

15. In a shallow pan, arrange seafood neatly. Heat on the table. Start with *tofu* pieces and end with oysters and Japanese parsley.

35

2 croakers (1 lb, 450g)
12 oz (340g) *tofu*
2 green onions or ½ onion
1²/₅ oz (40g) mushrooms
¼ bunch chrysanthemum leaves or
    watercress
4 cups *dashi* stock (See P94)
1²/₅ oz (40g) KOCHU JANG (hot sauce—
    See P95)
A { ¼ cup soy sauce
{ 1½ T *sake*
{ 1 t crushed garlic

∗ It is important to add fish after the
liquid is at boiling point, or the soup
will remain fishy.

This nourishing dish is one of Korea's most popular.

1. Remove scales and entrails from croakers. Cut up with bones attached.

2. Cut large mushrooms in half.

3. Cut *tofu* into 3, then into ½ in (1.5cm) slices.

4. Cut green onion diagonally. If using onion, cut into ⅛ in (0.3cm) slices.

5. Discard hard stems of chrysanthemum leaves. Use leaf part.

6. Heat *dashi* stock to boiling. Add fish and cook over medium heat, constantly skimming.

7. When fish is heated through, stir KOCHU JANG (hot sauce) into liquid and season with **A**.

8. Add vegetables in order (2), (3), then (4). When heated through, add chrysanthemum leaves.

INGREDIENTS: 4 servings

2 squid (9 oz, 250g)
5 oz (140g) boiled bamboo shoot
1¾ oz (50g) mushrooms
3 green peppers
¼ medium onion
3 green onions
1 T salad oil

A {
⅔ oz (20g) KOCHU JANG (hot sauce–See P95)
1 T sake
2 t soy sauce
1 t sugar
1 t ground chili pepper
½ t crushed garlic
Pepper
MSG
}

1 t roasted sesame seeds
½ t sesame oil

Korean version of stir-fried food with spicy hot sauce.

1. Prepare squid as directed on P 34. Tear off triangular "hat".

2. Rub the end surface with a kitchen cloth to catch the skin. Peel the skin from the body and "hat".

3. Cut body in half on skin side, then score in a diamond pattern.

4. Cut into 1 in (2.5cm) width.

5. Cut green peppers into quarters lengthwise. Cut bamboo shoot and onion into ⅛ in (0.3cm) width, green onion into 2 in (5cm) length.

6. Heat oil in a skillet, cook squid, bamboo shoot and onion over medium heat.

7. Add mushrooms and green peppers. When all ingredients are heated through, stir in green onion.

8. Season with **A**. Sprinkle with roasted sesame seeds and stir-fry quickly. Pour sesame oil rolling around the sides of skillet. Transfer to serving plate.

INGREDIENTS: 2 servings

1 sea bream (10½ oz, 300g)
⅔ oz (20g) carrot
1 green pepper
⅔ oz (20g) mushrooms
2 small green peppers
10 ginkgo nuts, boiled
⅔ oz (20g) ginger root

A { 1 T sake
1/4 t salt
Pepper

Dip
{ 1 T YANG NYEOM JANG (See P95)
1/2 T vinegar

* Omit vinegar from the dip, if you prefer.

This recipe reflects the Chinese influence with the use of fresh ginger root.

1. Scrape off scales of sea bream. Remove entrails through the gill. Rinse in water and pat-dry. Make several incisions on both sides.

2. Cut carrot into 2 in (5 cm) julienne strips.

3. Cut green pepper into halves, remove seeds, then cut into julienne strips.

4. Cut off hard stems from mushrooms and small green peppers. Peel ginger skin and slice thinly.

5. Lay 12 in (30cm) × 20 in (50cm) foil and place sea bream in center. Fold up foil along belly side and back side.

6. Fold up remaining sides alike to surround the fish.

7. Sprinkle with **A**. Top with sliced ginger. Join sides of foil to prevent dripping.

8. Place (7) in a steamer and steam over high heat for 10 minutes. Open foil and place carrot, green pepper, mushrooms and ginkgo nuts on top. Tightly close the foil again, and cook a further 5 minutes. Combine dip ingredients and serve in a small bowl.

Spicy/sour sauce makes this dish special.

INGREDIENTS: 4 servings

4 croakers
Salt

A ⎰ 4 T YANG NYEOM JANG (See P95)
  ⎱ 1 T vineger
    1 t finely chopped hot green pepper
    1 t finely chopped green onion
Lemon wedges, red leaf lettuce, parsley for garnish

* Croakers, bony fish from the Sciaenidae family, are caught in

The Atlantic near southern part of West Coast. They are best in early spring and summer, rich in protein and lipids.

* To make dip, blend YANG NYEOM JANG and vinegar in the 4:1 ratio.

* **Salt Coating:** When grilling whole fish, this easy technique is uesd to preserve the skin of fish. Sprinkle salt over the fish and let stand for a while. When salt is nearly absorbed, pat-dry the moisture. Grill over high direct fire and the surface of fish is coated with white grains of salt.

1. Scrape off scales. Discard entrails and wash in water quickly. Pat-dry, and make 3–4 incisions on both sides. Generously sprinkle salt over both sides.

2. On center shelf of oven preheated to 400°F (200°C), broil until the surface turns light brown, approx 5–8 minutes.

3. Combine **A** and pour over the fish. Reduce heat to 325°F (160°C) and broil a further 5 minutes. Transfer to serving plate and garnish with lettuce, parsley and lemon wedges.

CLAM BAKE 조개찜 *(Choge Chim)*

Garlic enhances the flavor of this clam bake; try it while still hot.

INGREDIENTS: 4 servings

1 lb (450g) short neck clams in shell
⅓ cup *sake*

A ⎰ 1 T finely chopped green onion
　　2 t soy sauce
　　1 t *mirin*
　　1 t finely chopped garlic
　　1 t roasted sesame seeds
　　Salt and pepper
　⎱ MSG

1 t sesame oil
2 stalks chives, finely chopped for garnish
Chili pepper, shredded for garnish

* Sand in clams spoils the flavor. Be sure to soak them in salted water.
* If you prefer hotter taste, cook with ground chili pepper.

1. Soak short neck clams in salt water as for sea water and set aside to remove sand. In a skillet, put clams and pour over *sake*. Cover and steam over high heat.

2. Steam 2–3 minutes until shells open. Combine all **A** ingredients and stir in. Sprinkle with sesame oil. Transfer to serving bowl and garnish with finely chopped chives and shredded chili pepper.

INGREDIENTS: 4 servings

12 clams in shell

A {
2 cups water
²/₃ cup *sake*
¹/₄ t salt
}

2 eggs, separated
3 dried *shiitake* mushrooms, soaked in water

B {
¹/₃ t soy sauce
Dash *mirin*, salt and pepper
Roasted sesame seeds
}

2 stalks chives, chopped finely
Chili pepper, shredded for garnish
Salad oil, salt

Dip
{
1 clove garlic
5 T soy sauce
3 T *mirin*
3 T roasted sesame seeds
}

This colorful platter is elegantly arranged to resemble a flower blossom.

1. Stir egg yolks and sprinkle with salt to taste. Grease a square omelet pan (wipe off excess oil with paper towel). Pour in yolks and rotate pan to cover the bottom.

2. When surface is nearly dry, separate edges with a skewer. Insert skewer through center to raise the omelet and turn. Cook only lightly.

3. Cut into 1¹/₂ in (4cm) width.

4. Shred finely. Cook and shred egg whites in the same manner.

5. Cut *shiitake* mushrooms thinly. Sauté in hot oil and season with **B**.

6. In a pan combine **A**, place clams so that they do not overlap. Cover and cook until shells open. (If the pan is small, separate clams in two.)

7. In a small saucepan, heat soy sauce, *mirin* and sesame seeds to boiling point. Add finely chopped garlic and immediately remove from heat.

8. Pour (7) sauce over clams. Garnish with mushrooms, omelet, chives and shredded chili pepper.

41

It can be prepared in minutes.

INGREDIENTS: 4 servings

$^1\!/_5$ oz (6g) dried *wakame* seaweed,
  soaked in water
2 oz (60g) shucked short neck clams
4 green onions

A {
  1 oz (30g) KOCHU JANG (hot
    sauce—See P95)
  1 T vinegar
  2 t sesame oil
  $1^1\!/_2$ t sugar
  1 t soy sauce
  1 t roasted sesame seeds
  $^1\!/_2$ t crushed garlic
}

Ground chili pepper
MSG

* Canned clams can be also used. If using
  frozen clams, cook when partially thawed.
* Substitute clams for oysters. Use only
  fresh oysters in shell. Blanch in boiling
  water until the surface turns whitish; cool
  in iced water and drain.

1. Cut *wakame* seaweed into 1 in
(2.5cm). Wash clams in salted water and
cook in boiling water; drain. Cut green
onion into $1^1\!/_2$ in (4cm) and cook briefly
in salted boiling water; drain.

2. In a bowl, put clams. Combine **A**
and pour over, mix well to season.

¼ lb (115g) each short neck clams and mussels
3 oz (85g) each shrimp, scallops, squid
2 oz (60g) white meat fish
1 oz (30g) red–purple seaweed, if available
½ bunch red leaf lettuce
1 oz (30g) chrysanthemum leaves
¼ onion, thinly sliced
½ cucumber, thinly sliced
½ green onion, thinly sliced
Dash white wine

Dressing
4 T soy sauce
2 T each sesame oil and vinegar
1 T sugar
2 t ground chili pepper
2 t roasted sesame seeds
1 t crushed garlic
Dash pepper, white wine, lemon juice and MSG

This dish is appropriate for festive occasions. It is elegant enough to be served as a main course.

1. Prepare seafood. See directions on bottom right of this page.

2. Discard hard stems of chrysanthemum leaves. Soak sliced onion, cucumber, green onion and chrysanthemum leaves in iced water to get crisp texture.

3. Tear red leaf lettuce into bite size pieces and place in another bowl.

4. Drain (2) and add to the lettuce. Combine dressing ingredients and pour half over vegetable; toss well.

5. Into remaining dressing, add all seafood but red purple seaweed. Rub the dressing into seafood. In serving bowl, place tossed vegetables, then arrange seasoned seafood. Top with red-purple seaweed in center.

DIRECTIONS

* **Clams, Mussels:** Soak in salt water as for sea water for a while to remove sand. Scrub the shells and cook covered, with white wine sprinkled over, until shells open.
* **Shrimp:** Cook in salted boiling water briefly; shell.
* **Scallops:** Insert a knife between shells and pry open. Separate flesh from shell using sharp utensil. Cook briefly in salted boiling water.
* **Squid:** Remove tentacles and entrails (See P 34). Peel skin and slice. Blanch in boiling water.
* **Red-purple seaweed:** Wash thoroughly and cut into bite size pieces.
* **White meat fish:** Cook in salted boiling water. Cut into bite size pieces.

ASSORTED VEGETABLES 나물 *(Namool)*

Toasted sesame seeds bring a distinctive flavor to this dish.

INGREDIENTS: 4 servings

1 bunch spinach

A
- 1 T minced green onion
- 1 T sesame oil
- ½ t salt
- ½ ground sesame seeds

¼ *daikon* radish (9 oz, 250g)
2 oz (60g) carrot
¼ t salt

B
- 1 T vinegar
- 2 t sugar
- 2 t ground sesame seeds
- 1 t crushed garlic
- 1 t mined green onion
- ¼ t ground chili pepper

10½ oz (300g) soybean sprouts

C
- 1 T sesame oil
- 2 t minced green onion
- 1½ t ground sesame seeds
- 1 t crushed garlic
- ½ t salt

7 oz (200g) fiddlehead, cooked
1 T sesame oil

1 t crushed garlic

D
- 2 T soy sauce
- 1 T minced green onion
- 2 t each *sake* and *mirin*

1 t ground sesame seeds
Salt

* NAMOOL is a general term for salads prepared in Korean fashion. Salads with cooked vegetables are called SUKCHE while raw vegetable salads are called SENGCHE. Usually NAMOOL means SUKCHE. Whether they are boiled or stir-fried depends on ingredients, but in any case the key to the "Korean flavor" lies in a generous use of sesame oil and sesame seeds.

* When sesame seeds are used for dressings, grind lightly so they do not slip off the vegetables.

1. Wash spinach well and cook in salted boiling water briefly over high heat, blanch in cold water. Squeeze excess water.

2. Cut into 1½ in (4cm) length.

3. Combine **A**. Add spinach and mix by hand rubbing the seasoning into the spinach.

4. Peel *daikon* radish. Slice thinly and then into 2 in (5cm) julienne strips.

5. Peel carrot and cut as with *daikon* radish.

6. In a bowl, place (4) and (5). Sprinkle with ¼ t salt and let stand 10 minutes. Lightly squeeze out water.

7. Combine **B**. Add (6) and mix with hand rubbing the seasoning into the vegetables.

8. Discard roots of soybean sprouts. Wash and place in a pan. Add enough water to cover and a pinch of salt, cover and cook over medium heat 10 minutes. When the smell of cooked beans comes out, drain and cool. Combine **C** and season.

9. Drain fiddlehead. Heat sesame oil in a pan, add fiddlehead and stir-fry. Add **D** to taste. Boil down and sprinkle with ground sesame seeds.

MIXED VEGETABLES WITH BEEF 잡채 (Chapche)

An assortment of vegetables is artfully garnished with egg strips.

INGREDIENTS: 4 servings

5 oz (150 g) lean beef

A {
2 T soy sauce
1 T sesame oil
1 t each sugar and *sake*
½ t *mirin*
Crushed garlic, roasted sesame seeds, finely chopped green onion
}

1¾ oz (50 g) bean threads
1 green onion
4 dried *shiitake* mushrooms, soaked in water
1 oz (30 g) carrot

⅓ oz (10 g) dried cloud ear mushrooms, soaked in water
1 green pepper
⅔ t salad oil
Salt and pepper

B {
1 t roasted sesame seeds
⅔ t soy sauce
½ t sugar
⅓ t sesame oil
Crushed garlic, pepper, MSG
}

Shredded omelet (See P94)

1. In salted boiling water, cook bean threads 3–4 minutes until transparent. Remove from heat.

2. Drain and cut into 2½ in (6.5 cm) length.

3. Cut beef into julienne strips.

4. In a bowl combine **A** and add beef to marinate.

46

5. Slice green onion diagonally.

6. Remove stems of *shiitake* mushrooms and cut into julienne strips.

7. Cut ear mushrooms into bite size pieces. Cut carrot and green pepper into julienne strips.

8. Heat salad oil in a skillet, and add green onion. Cook briefly and season with salt and pepper. In the same manner cook all vegetables.

9. Heat salad oil in a skillet and cook beef strips.

10. In a bowl combine **B**. Add bean threads and mix well.

11. Add vegetables and beef. Mix lightly and transfer to serving bowl. Garnish with shredded omelet.

◄ VARIATION ► **MIXED VEGETABLES WITH SEAFOOD** 해물잡채 (*Haemul Chapche*)

INGREDIENTS: 4 servings

Fresh ingredients are the key to this dish.

3 oz (85 g) shrimp, shelled
3 oz (85 g) squid
3 oz (85 g) scallops
2 oz (60 g) shucked short neck clams
Vegetables prepared as above
Parsley for garnish

1. Remove tentacles and entrails from squid. Peel skin and slice. Separate scallop flesh from shell. Rinse shellfish in salted water.

2. In salted boiling water cook briefly and drain in a colander; let stand to cool.

3. Prepare vegetables as illustrated in the process above, (1), (2), (5)–(8), (10), (11). Mix lightly with seafood.

Quickly sautéed mushrooms can be accompanied by main dish or compliment to party menu.

INGREDIENTS: 4 servings

4 oz (115g) *shimeji* mushrooms
2 oz (60g) *enokitake* mushrooms
2 oz (60g) *shiitake* mushrooms
6 button mushrooms
2 oz (60g) green onions
¼ lb (115g) lean beef

A { ¼ t crushed garlic
    { Salt and pepper

B { ¼ cup beef stock (See P94)
    { ½ t salt
    { ½ t *sake*
    { Pepper
    { MSG

1 T salad oil
Chili pepper, shredded for garnish
Roasted sesame seeds for garnish

* If fresh *shiitake* mushrooms are not available, use dried ones soaked in water. Cloud ear mushrooms can be added for more flavor.
* It is important to cook mushrooms only briefly over high heat to preserve full flavor and liquor.

1. Discard root of *shimeji* mushrooms and separate into small sections. Discard 1 in (2.5cm) root of *enokitake* mushrooms. Discard stems of *shiitake* mushrooms and cut into halves or quarters. Clean button mushrooms and slice thinly. Cut green onion into 1 in (2.5cm) length.

2. Heat salad oil in a skillet and cook beef over high heat. Season with **A**.

3. Stir in mushrooms. When heated through and flexible, Pour over **B** and bring to a boil. Transfer to serving plate, garnish with ground chili pepper and roasted sesame seeds.

The introduction of garlic stalks excite health-nutrition conscious people.

INGREDIENTS: 4 servings

5 oz (140g) garlic stalks
4 oz (115g) *shimeji* mushrooms
6 button mushrooms
¼ lb (115g) lean beef
Salt and pepper

A
1 T soy sauce
2 t sugar
1 t *sake*
1 t *mirin*
¼ t crushed garlic
Pepper

1 T salad oil

¼ t sesame oil
Roasted sesame seeds

*Garlic stalks are available in frozen style too. Although lacking in flavor and texture, frozen garlic stalks are very useful for emergency appetizers.

1. Cut garlic stalks into 1½ in (4cm) length. Separate *shimeji* mushrooms into small sections. Clean button mushrooms and slice finely. Cut beef into julienne strips.

2. Heat salad oil and add beef. Cook and stir over high heat. Season with salt and pepper.

3. Add garlic stalks and stir-fry briefly. Stir in mushrooms. When heated through, season with **A**, and bring to a boil. Sprinkle with sesame oil. Transfer to serving plate and garnish with roasted sesame seeds.

INGREDIENTS: 4 servings

4 small cucumbers (14 oz, 400g)
5¼ oz (150g) lean beef
1 t salt
1 T salad oil

A { ¼ t crushed garlic
{ Salt and pepper

B { 1 T finely chopped green onion
{ 1 t roasted sesame seeds
{ 1 t sesame oil
{ ½ t soy sauce
{ ½ t ground chili pepper
{ ¼ t salt

Chili pepper, shredded

*Stir-fry quickly or the cucumber will lose its texture.

Beef and cucumbers are transformed into a legendary Korean delicacy.

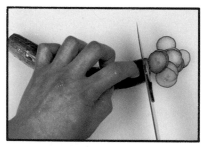

1. Cut off both ends of cucumbers and slice thinly.

2. In a bowl place cucumbers and sprinkle with 1 t salt; let stand 5–10 minutes.

3. When cucumbers are flexible, wrap in a cloth or paper towel and squeeze out water.

4. Cut beef into julienne strips.

5. Heat salad oil. Quickly stir-fry beef over high heat and season with **A**.

6. Add cucumber slices and stir-fry briefly. Season with **B**. Transfer to serving plate and garnish with shredded chili pepper.

Toasted sesame seeds impart a rich aroma to this dish.

INGREDIENTS: 4 servings

20 small green peppers (2½ oz, 70g)
Flour for dusting
Salad oil for greasing steamer

A {
3 T soy sauce
1 t vinegar
½ t sesame oil
½ t sugar
½ t roasted sesame seeds
¼ t ground chili pepper
Crushed garlic
MSG
}

* The Koreans usually use young hot green peppers which have not developed their real sharpness, for this dish.
* Greasing the bottom of steamer prevents the green peppers from sticking.
* This makes a very good appetizer and goes very well with alcohol. Make in quantity and refrigerate for emergency. Keeps a week in refrigerator.

1. Wash and pat-dry small green peppers. Discard stems.

2. Lightly dust with flour.

3. In a prepared steamer, place peppers. Steam over high heat 5–6 minutes; cool.

4. In a bowl combine **A**. Add peppers and mix well.

This hearty potato dish is enhanced with sesame oil, traditional Korean seasoning for many centuries.

INGREDIENTS: 4 servings

5 potatoes (1¾ lbs, 800g)
7 oz (700g) boneless beef rib
3 dried *shiitake* mushrooms, soaked in water
5 small green peppers
2 T salad oil
A { 1 t ground chili pepper
{ ½ t crushed garlic
Cooking Sauce
{ 2 cups beef stock (See P94)
{ 3 T soy sauce
{ 2 T sake
{ ⅔ T sugar
{ ¼ T mirin

1 t sesame oil
White part of green onion for garnish
Chili pepper, shredded for garnish

* Watch carefully. Potatoes crumble easily.

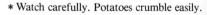

1. Slice potatoes into ½ in (1.5cm). Soak in water to remove starch; drain. Cut beef into 1½ in (4cm) long rectangles. Discard stems of mushrooms and cut, if necessary. Discard stems of small green peppers.

2. Heat salad oil, add potatoes and beef. Stir-fry over high heat and add **A**.

3. Combine all cooking sauce ingredients, add to the pan. Cook over medium heat until the sauce has reduced by half. Add mushrooms and continue to cook. Stir in small green pepper, immediately remove from heat. Pour sesame oil rolling around the sides of pan. Serve garnished with shredded green onion and shredded chili pepper.

This dish has a tasty and exotic Oriental flavor.

INGREDIENTS: 4 servings

½ *daikon* radish (18 oz, 500g)
7 oz (200g) chicken breast
2 chili peppers
1 T salad oil
½ t crushed garlic
Cooking Sauce
2 cups beef stock (See P94)
3 T soy sauce
2 T *sake*
1 T sugar
¼ t *mirin*
Pepper

1 t sesame oil
Chrysanthemum leaves (optional)
Shredded omelet (See P94)

* If you prefer richer flavor, substitute with chicken thigh.
* The more in quantity, the richer in taste. Warm and serve remainder next day, as the sauce will seep through, enhancing the flavor.

1. Peel *daikon* radish and cut into ½ in (1.5cm) halfmoons. Cut chicken into 1 in (2.5cm) cubes. Soak chili peppers in vinegared, lukewarm water; chop.

2. Heat oil and add *daikon* radish and chicken. Stir-fry over high heat. Stir in chopped chili peppers and crushed garlic.

3. Add all cooking sauce ingredients and cook over medium heat, constantly skimming. Pour sauce over occasionally. When all the sauce has nearly evaporated, sprinkle sesame oil. Remove from heat and serve, garnished with chrysanthemum leaves and shredded omelet.

STUFFED CABBAGE ROLLS 캬베츠말이 *(Cabbage Sam)*

The secret of this colorful and nourishing fillings is *tofu* and dried baby shrimp.

INGREDIENTS: 4 servings

8 cabbage leaves
1/3 oz (10 g) dried shrimp
12 oz (340 g) firm *tofu*, drained
  (See P60)
3 medium dried *shiitake* mushrooms, soaked in water

A
{
1 T flour
1 t sesame oil
1 t roasted sesame seeds
1/2 t salt
1/2 egg, beaten
Pepper
}

3 1/2 cups beef stock (See P94)

B
{
2 t sake
1 1/2 t salt
Soy sauce
}

* Adjust the amount of beef stock to
  the size of pan so the cabbage rolls
  are always covered.
* Cabbage leaves can be cooked in
  steamer, 15 minutes over high
  heat.

1. In salted boiling water, cook cabbage leaves, heart end first.

2. Immediately blanch in cold water; drain on a colander. Slice off thick part.

3. In a bowl place dried shrimp. Add boiling water to cover, let stand 4–5 minutes.

4. Tightly squeeze out water. Discard hard stems of mushrooms and chop finely. Drain *tofu* well.

5. Put in a bowl and add **A** ingredients.

6. Blend well until smooth.

7. Place ⅛ portion onto each cabbage leaf.

8. Roll towards far end, then fold in sides.

9. Roll up tightly.

10. Roll up with the remainder. Makes 8.

11. In a large and shallow pan or a skillet, add beef stock. Place cabbage rolls, rolled ends down. Bring to a boil over medium heat, then reduce heat. Cook 15 minutes and add **B**. Simmer a further 5 minutes.

SEAFOOD AND VEGETABLE OMELET 전 *(Cheon)*

This egg battered dish is one of the most popular in Korea.

INGREDIENTS: 4 servings

8 large shrimp
8 large oysters
5 oz (140 g) white meat fish fillets
    such as cod, swordfish
6 oz (170 g) firm *tofu*
⅛ pumpkin (4 oz, 115 g)
Salt and pepper
½ cup flour for dusting
Batter
⌈ 2 whole eggs and 1 yolk
| 1 t salt
| 1 t crushed garlic
⌊ MSG and pepper
Salad oil

* This dish is a must in Korean ceremonies and parties. The ingredients are dusted with flour, dipped into lightly mixed eggs, then cooked in hot oil being pressed down to the pan. This traditional method lets the moisture escape and thicken the flavor. Prepared with only salt and pepper, it is eaten with vinegared soy sauce.
* Try any kind of ingredients. Cut vegetables and meats into thin slices. Cut fish into bite size pieces.

1. Shell shrimp. Cut open along the back, and devein.

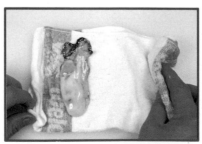

2. Wash oysters in salted water and pat-dry. Cut fish fillets into ¼ in (0.7 cm) slices.

3. Wrap *tofu* in a cloth and top with a chopping board; let stand to drain, 30 minutes. Cut into ½ in (1.5 cm) thickness. Cut pumpkin into thin slices.

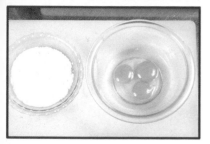

4. In a bowl, mix batter ingredients.

5. Lightly dust with flour.

6. Shake off excess flour.

7. Heat oil in a skillet. Dip ingredients into (4) and place in skillet. Cook both sides.

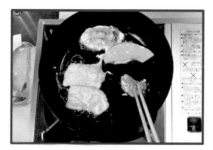

8. When cooking, press out water using fork. Arrange on serving plate and serve with vinegared soy sauce.

◀ VARIATION ▶ **KEBAB KOREAN STYLE** 꼬치전(*Kochi Cheon*)

INGREDIENTS: 4 servings

7 oz (200g) beef steak
4 white parts of green onion
3 oz (85g) white part of CHINESE CAB-
   BAGE KIMCHEE (See P80)
4 small green peppers
Salt and pepper
1/2 cup flour for dusting
Batter
  { 2 whole eggs and 1 yolk
  { 1 t each salt and crushed garlic
  { Pepper and MSG
Salad oil

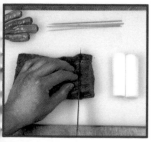

1. Cut all vegetables into 3 in (8cm) length. Cut beef into 1/2 in (1.5cm) width and 3 in (8cm) length. Rince KIM-CHEE in water. Remove stems of small green peppers.

2. Arrange in a row; green onion, beef, KIMCHEE, small green pepper, beef, ending with green onion. Skewer through sides, then center. Season to taste with salt and pepper.

3. In a skillet heat enough oil to prevent sticking. Pre-fry both sides over medium heat, 1 minute each.

4. Dust both sides with flour. Dip into batter and fry over medium heat until heated through. Cut between skewers and serve.

6 eggs, beaten

A { Dash sugar
{ Dash salt

2 oz (60g) beef steak

B { 1 T soy sauce
{ ½ T sesame oil
{ ½ t sugar
{ ½ sake
{ ¼ t mirin
{ Crushed garlic, roasted sesame
{   seeds, minced green onion

2 oz (60g) carrot, shredded
2 medium dried *shiitake* mushrooms,
   soaked in water
2 oz (60g) seasoned spinach (See P 44)
2 sheets *nori* seaweed
Salad oil
Parsley

A simple omelet can be turned into an elegant side dish.

1. Season eggs with **A**. Cut beef into julienne strips and marinate in **B**. Shred *shiitake* mushrooms. Stir-fry each ingredient in hot oil; set aside.

2. Heat square omelet pan and grease over the bottom; wipe off excess. Pour in ⅓ amount of egg mixture.

3. Just before the surface dries, place roasted *nori* seaweed trimmed a little smaller than the pan. Remove from heat.

4. Put half amount of meat and vegetables on far end.

5. Pour in ¼ amount of egg mixture along near end.

6. Inserting a sharp utensil and holding by hand, roll from far end. When rolled to half, return to low heat.

7. Roll up and transfer to a bamboo mat or towel; press lightly to shape and cool.

8. Cut into eating pieces and arrange in a dish. Garnish with parsley.

8 small eggs
{ 2 cups *dashi* stock (See P94)
{ 2 T salted opposum shrimp (See P107)
4 shrimp, deveined
1²/₅ oz (40g) mushrooms
1 salted cod roe
4 stalks Japanese parsley
Soy sauce
Chili pepper, shredded for garnish

* A large size bowl can be used for 4 portions. If adding all ingredients at a time, steam over low heat 20–30 minutes until a skewer inserted halfway comes out with no liquid.
* Use salted opposum shrimp only to add flavor. Strain off and use only the liquor.

The custard-like texture has a delicate flavor.

1. Rinse shrimp in small amount of soy sauce; pat-dry.

2. Shred mushrooms. Cut cod roe into bite size pieces. Cut Japanese parsley into 1 in (2.5 cm) length.

3. Lightly beat eggs, but do not whisk. Add *dashi* stock and salted opposum shrimp. Stir well and strain through a fine strainer.

4. Into 4 serving bowls with lids, pour in egg mixture. Add mushrooms and Japanese parsley.

5. In a hot steamer place the bowls and cook over low heat 7 minutes. Add shrimp and cod roe and steam a further 10 minutes. Sprinkle with shredded chili pepper, if desired.

INGREDIENTS: 4 servings

24 oz (685g) firm *tofu*
{ Salt and pepper
{ Flour for dusting
1 T salad oil
1 chili pepper
2 T YANG NYEOM JANG (See P95)
Enokitake mushrooms, small green
    peppers, CHINESE CABBAGE KIM-
    CHEE (See P80) for garnish
Chives, chopped

* *Tofu*-draining time depends on the
type of dish, but generally it is pressed
down to ⅔ thickness. A chopping
board makes an ideal weight.
* Soak dried chili pepper in lukewarm
water with a few drops of vinegar
ahead of time.

Sautéed *tofu* can be something special with a sauce.

1. Wrap *tofu* in a cloth
and press under a 4 lbs
(1.5kg) weight 20–30
minutes.

2. Cut in half, then into
half thickness.

3. Sprinkle salt and pep-
per over one side.

4. Coat with flour on all
sides.

5. Shake off excess flour.

6. Heat oil in a skillet and
add *tofu*. Cook over
medium heat.

7. Cook on both sides un-
til golden brown.

8. Spoon over chopped chili pepper and YANG NYEOM JANG;
remove from heat. Sauté garnish
ingredients of your chioce and
season with salt and pepper.
Transfer to a warmed plate and
sprinkle with chopped chives, if
desired.

***Tofu* has gained international popularity among gourmets in recent years. This dish is another attractive way to serve *tofu*.**

INGREDIENTS: 4 servings

24 oz (685g) firm *tofu*
2 oz (60g) beef for steak
2 green onion
2 T salad oil
Cooking Sauce
{ ½ cup beef stock (See P94)
2 T soy sauce
1 T sugar
2 t sake
1 t crushed garlic
1 t ground chili pepper
MSG
1 T sesame oil

* Use any cut of beef.

1. Drain *tofu* (See P60). Cut in half and then into ½ in (1.5cm) thickness. Cut beef into thin slices. Cut green onion into 1½ in (4cm) length.

2. Heat oil in a skillet and add *tofu*. Cook over medium heat until brown and crisp on both sides.

3. In a saucepan combine cooking sauce ingredients. Add *tofu* and beef, cook over medium heat. Occasionally shake pan so cooking sauce covers ingredients.

4. When cooking sauce has reduced by half, add green onion. When cooking sauce is barely visible, sprinkle on sesame oil and remove from heat.

INGREDIENTS: 4 servings

24 oz (685g) firm *tofu*
1 bunch green onion (12–16 stalks)
7 oz (200g) ground beef

A
- 1 T soy sauce
- 1 T finely chopped green onion
- ½ t crushed garlic
- ½ t sesame oil
- 1 egg, beaten
- Pepper

4 oz (115g) *daikon* radish, cut into quarters and sliced
1 oz (30g) carrot, cut into strips
1⅖ oz (40g) mushrooms, sliced

Cooking Sauce
- 2 cups beef stock (See P94)
- ½ t each crushed garlic and salt
- ¼ t soy sauce

Shredded omelet (See P94), chili pepper, shredded, chrysanthemum leaves and salad oil

This is a Korean version of a hot pot and the flavor reflects the Chinese and Japanese influences.

1. Drain *tofu* (See P60). Cut in half, then into ¼ in (0.7cm) thickness. Cook green onion in salted boiling water; drain.

2. Heat oil in a skillet and add *tofu*. Cook over medium heat until brown on both sides; cool.

3. In a bowl combine ground meats and **A**. Blend well.

4. Make *tofu* sandwiches. Spoon meat mixture over slice of *tofu* and top with another slice.

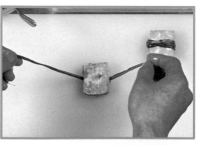

5. Bind sandwiches with green onion "strings" tightly. On bottom of fireproof casserole, lay *daikon* slices. Arrange *tofu* sandwiches. Pour over

cooking sauce ingredients. Cook over low heat until meat filling is done. Arrange carrot and mushrooms between *tofu* and bring to a boil. Remove from heat and garnish with shredded omelet, shredded chili pepper and chrysanthemum leaves.

INGREDIENTS: 4 servings

16 oz (450g) *tofu*
6 oz (170g) short neck clams in shell
4 oz (115g) beef cubes or slices
8 small green peppers or 4 green peppers
1 green onion
½ small onion
2 T sesame oil
A { 2 t ground chili pepper
      { ½ t crushed garlic
B { 3½ oz (100g) red *miso*
      { 2½ oz (70g) white *miso*
2 cups *dashi* stock (See P94)

∗ **Quick & Easy version:** After the process (3), transfer to a large fire-proof casserole, add *dashi* stock and remaining ingredients. Let everyone help themselves from the casserole.
∗ Soak clams in salt water like sea water overnight to remove sand.

Calcium rich *tofu* can be served at any meal.

1. Cut *tofu* into ½ in (1.5cm) thick eating pieces. Soak clams in salted water to remove sand. Discard stems of small green peppers. If using regular green pepper, discard the core and cut in quarters lengthwise. Cut green onion into 1 in (2.5cm) length, onion into wedges.

2. Heat 1 T sesame oil and cook beef and **A** until beef turns color.

3. Add **B**. Cook and stir over medium heat until *miso* starts to burn on surface of pan.

4. Pour in *dashi* stock and cook 10 minutes.

5. Add clams and continue to cook until shells open.

6. Add *tofu*, green peppers, green onion and onion. When heated through, sprinkle 1 T sesame oil and remove from heat. Transfer to warmed individual casseroles.

"BIBIMPAP", meat and seasoned vegetables arranged on rice are very popular.

INGREDIENTS: Per serving

1 cup cooked rice (See P92)
1 oz (30g) beef
Marinade
- ½ T soy sauce
- ⅔ t sesame oil
- ¼ t sugar
- ¼ t *mirin*
- Dash *sake*, crushed garlic, roasted sesame seeds

1 oz (30g) each *daikon* radish and carrot, spinach, soybean sprouts and fiddlehead, seasoned as directed on P44
1 egg
Salad oil

* This dish, BIBIMPAP is a popular treat on Buddhist or other festival evenings in Korea. It is served as a lunch too. Garnish with KOCHU JANG (hot sauce—See P 95)

* Fried egg mold is a plain, uninteresting mold, but it is very useful when making a thick perfect fried egg. Before using, grease inside.

1. Cut beef into strips and marinate 5 minutes. In hot oil cook briefly; set aside. Place hot cooked rice in serving bowl.

2. Arrange 4 kinds of seasoned vegetable on rice. Place beef in center.

3. Heat oil in a skillet and put 3 in (8 cm) circle mold. Drop egg and cook.

4. Place fried egg on top of beef. Serve with KOCHU JANG (hot sauce) and sesame oil in small dish. Mix everything when eating.

1 cup cooked rice (See P92)
2 oz (60g) *daikon* radish
½ green onion
1¼ cups beef stock (See P94)

A { ½ t salt / Pepper / MSG

1 egg
Chrysanthemum leaves or watercress

* This style dish—steaming hot soup poured over rice—is an ideal snack, especially after drinking. It has many variations and is made throughout Korea.
* Add spinach, bean sprouts or *wakame* seaweed, if desired.
* Less heavier taste than **COOKED RICE IN OXTAIL SOUP** (See P 15).

One of the easiest of all Korean dishes makes a fine light meal in a bowl.

1. Peel *daikon* radish.

2. Cut into thin quarter rounds.

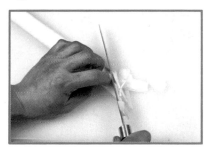

3. Cut green onion into thin diagonal slices.

4. In a saucepan over medium heat, add beef stock and *daikon* slices. Bring to a boil.

5. Add green onion and season with **A**. Pour in beaten egg, rolling slowly. When egg is nearly set, remove from heat.

6. Pour over hot rice. Garnish with chrysanthemum leaves and pepper.

This dish is easily digested for people who have over indulged or are out of sort.

3 cups cooked rice (See P92)
5 cups *dashi* stock (See P94)
2 oz (60g) *daikon* radish, cut into quarters and sliced
2 oz (60g) carrot, cut into quarters and sliced
¼ bunch spinach
¼ t salt
4 egg, yolks
YANG NYEOM JANG (See P95)

∗ Cook and serve in a large fire-proof casserole for the whole family.

1. Rinse cooked rice briefly in water to remove starch; drain. In a saucepan put rice and *dashi* stock, cook over medium heat.

2. Bring to a boil and reduce heat. Cook 3–4 minutes. Stir in *daikon* radish and carrot.

3. When vegetables are heated through, season with salt. Stir in spinach and remove from heat. Cover and let stand.

4. Transfer to individual serving bowl and drop egg yolk. Mix yolk and rice when eating. Season with YANG NYEOM JANG, if desired.

Rice recipes have become more popular throughout the world. Chicken goes well with rice.

INGREDIENTS: 4 servings

2 cups rice
{ 10 cups water
{ 2 cups chicken stock (See P94)
7 oz (200g) chicken breast
A { 1 T *sake* or white wine
{ Pinch of salt
YANG NYEOM JANG (See P95)
Green onion, chopped finely

* Mix as much green onion as you like with YANG NYEOM JANG, or add crushed garlic and ground chili pepper, if desired.
* For a richer flavor, substitute chicken breast for chicken thigh.
* The more the rice is stirred the more gluten it forms.

1. Wash rice and soak in 10 cups water for 1 hour.

2. Cut chicken into bite size pieces and marinate in **A** 10 minutes.

3. In a fire-proof casserole, cook rice with water over medium heat. Bring to a boil, stir in chicken stock, reduce heat. Cook until rice is very tender.

4. Add chicken and continue to cook just until heated through. Serve with YANG NYEOM JANG, mixed with chopped green onion.

A Korean version of rice pilaf. This dish gets its rich flavor from the clam and clam juice.

INGREDIENTS: 4 servings

3 cups rice
1 can short neck clams (8 oz, 225g)
7 oz (200g) soybean sprouts

A {
 3½ cups liquid from can plus water
 2 t sake
 1 t light soy sauce
 1 t salt
}

YANG NYEOM JANG (See P95)

* If using an electric rice cooker, add clams after the rice has cooked, and let steam longer with remaining heat.
* **Soybean sprouts:** Cultivated in the same way as regular bean sprouts, but 3–4 times larger in size, stronger against heat. They have crispier texture and more "bean" flavor which can be drawn out when cooked with rice. When cooking, boil in cold water covered to remove the "grassy" smell.

1. Wash rice and drain 30 minutes or longer. Drain short neck clams, reserving liquid. Discard roots from soybean sprouts and wash thoroughly.

2. Combine rice, **A** and soybean sprouts. Cook covered over high heat. Bring to a boil, then reduce heat to medium. Cook 5–6 minutes and reduce heat to low. Cook a further 5–6 minutes.

3. Stir in clams and simmer over very low heat 5 minutes. Remove from heat, fluff gently. Cover and let steam 5 minutes. Serve with YANG NYEOM JANG mixed with finely chopped green onion; blend when eating.

4 cups cooked rice (See P92)
4 oz (115g) lean beef
6 oz (170g) CHINESE CABBAGE KIMCHEE (See P80)
6 oz (170g) seasoned soybean sprouts (See P44)
1½ T each sesame oil and salad oil
Salt and pepper
Green onion, chopped finely
KOCHU JANG (hot sauce—See P95)

* Add green peppers or carrot, if desired.
* Stir-fry quickly over high heat. Do not cook over low heat as it spoils the rice texture.
* It is better to use hot rice as it does not form lumps while stir-frying.

This recipe is quite different from the fried rice we are familier with. KIMCHEE and beef provide an interesting texture and taste.

1. Cut beef into strips, and sprinkle with salt and pepper.

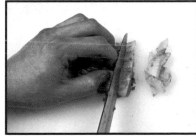

2. Cut KIMCHEE crosswise into ½ in (1.5cm) width.

3. Heat sesame oil and salad oil, and cook beef over high heat until it changes color.

4. Add rice and fluff gently.

5. Stir in KIMCHEE and seasoned soybean sprouts.

6. Cook and stir until rice has separated. Adjust the taste with salt and pepper. Transfer to serving dish and sprinkle with finely chopped green onion. Serve with KOCHU JANG (hot sauce), if desired.

ROLLED RICE WITH *NORI* SEAWEED 김밥 *(Kimbap)*

Assorted fillings make a colorful contrast.

INGREDIENTS: 4 servings (3 rolls)

3½ cups *sushi* rice (See ✳)
3 sheets roasted *nori* seaweed
5 oz (140g) lean beef

A {
2 T soy sauce
1 T sesame oil
1 t each sugar and *sake*
½ t *mirin*
Crushed garlic, roasted sesame seeds, finely chopped green onion
}

1 small cucumber
2 oz (60g) carrot
7 dried *shiitake* mushrooms
2 eggs, beaten

B {
1 t each *sake* and sugar
¼ t salt
}
Salad oil, salt and pepper

✳ HOW TO MAKE *SUSHI* RICE

Ingredients: 3½ cups cooked rice
Vinegar Mixture (3 T vinegar   1 T sugar   1 t salt)

Directions: Put cooked rice into mixing tub and sprinkle vinegar mixture generously over rice. With a large wooden spoon, mix with a slicing motion. While you mix, have a helper, (electric fan). This is not to cool *sushi* rice, but to puff the extra liquid away.

1. Cut beef into strips.

2. Combine **A**; add beef to marinate.

3. Halve cucumber lengthwise, then cut into thin diagonal slices. Sprinkle with salt, let stand until soft; squeeze out water.

4. Cut carrot into 2 in (5cm) long strips.

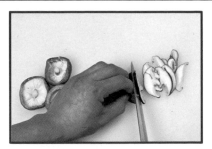

5. Soak dried *shiitake* mushrooms in lukewarm water until soft. Discard stems and slice thinly.

6. Heat salad oil in a skillet and cook beef over high heat; set aside. Likewise stir-fry each ingredient lightly and season with salt and pepper.

7. Mix egg and **B** well. Pour over lightly greased square omelet pan thinly.

8. When half-set, roll from far side tightly. When golden brown, remove from heat.

9. Cut lengthwise in three.

10. Lay *nori* seaweed over bamboo mat. Spoon over 1/3 amount (1 1/6 cups) evenly. Wet your fingers with vinegared water and press gently.

11. Leave 1/2 in (1.5cm) on your side, 1 in (2.5cm) on far side uncoverd.

12. Arrange beef, cucumber, mushrooms, carrot and egg omelet in contrasting colors slightly below center.

13. Holding edges of fillings, roll in one motion so the uncovered *nori* seaweed meet each other.

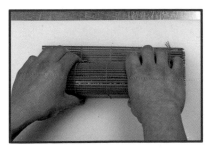

14. Roll up and shape. Press ends.

15. Cut each roll into 8. Wipe the knife with wet cloth after each slice. Arrange on a plate cut side up.

COLD NOODLE DISH 냉면 *(Nengmyeon)*

Buckwheat noodles are particularly tasty and refreshing during the hot summer months.

INGREDIENTS: 4 servings

21 oz (600 g) dried Korean noodles
Soup
- 14 oz (400 g) beef for soup (shank, brisket etc)
- 1 clove garlic, thinly sliced
- 1 oz (30 g) ginger root, thinly sliced
- 2 green parts of green onion
- 1 chili pepper
- 3 T vinegar
- 1½ T soy sauce
- ¼ t peppercorns

1 cucumber
- Salt, 3% weight of cucumber
- 1 T vinegar
- MSG

¼ *daikon* radish
- Salt, 3% weight of radish
- 1 T vinegar
- ½ t ground chili pepper
- ⅓ t ginger juice
- Crushed garlic
- Dash sugar

2 eggs, hard boiled (See P12)
2 oz (60 g) braised beef (**COUNTRY STYLE BEEF**–See P12)
¼ apple or pear
Seasonings for Soup
- 3 T vinegar
- 2½ t salt
- 2½ t sugar
- 2 t MSG
- 1 beef bouillon cube

* When making soup, add beef knuckle (above-right in picture) if available.
* This is everyone's favorite dish in Korea.

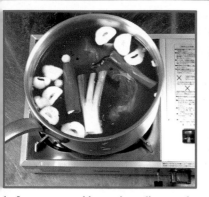

1. In saucepan add soup ingredients and 3 quarts (3 lit) water. Bring to a boil over high heat; reduce heat and simmer covered 3 hours, frequently skimming.

2. Strain through a fine strainer. The soup has reduced to 7 cups. Heat to boiling again; remove surface fat with paper towel. Refrigerate 2–3 hours; remove all fat.

3. Halve cucumber lengthwise.

4. Slice diagonally.

5. Peel *daikon* radish and cut into 1/8 in (0.3 cm) thick rectangles.

6. Sprinkle (4) and (5) with salt and let stand 5–6 minutes. Lightly rinse and squeeze out water. Mix in remaining seasonings.

7. Halve hard boiled eggs. Cut braised beef into 1/4 in (0.7 cm) thickness. Slice apple or pear thinly.

8. In boiling water cook noodles 2–3 minutes.

9. Rinse in cold running water to remove gluten; drain. Heat (2) and seasonings, bring to a boil; cool. In chilled bowl, place noodles, apple, cucumber, *daikon* radish, sliced beef and boiled egg. Pour over chilled soup. Serve with vinegar and mustard, if desired.

HOT NOODLE DISH 온면 *(Onmyeon)*

This enchanting combination of noodles and vegetables can be served as a light lunch.

INGREDIENTS: 4 servings

18 oz (500g) dried Korean noodles
5 oz (140g) beef
2 green peppers
1²/₅ oz (40g) mushrooms
½ each onion and green onion
¼ bunch chrysanthemum leaves
3½ cups beef stock (See P94)
A { 2½ t salt
2 t soy sauce
Crushed garlic
2 eggs
Finely chopped green onion
Pepper

* Noodles should be served immediately after draining. Watch the soup cooking time when starting to cook noodles.
* Korean noodles are made mainly from buckwheat. Flour or potato starch is added to give smoothness. There are slight differences of ingredients according to the region. There are also many shapes and sizes, just like spaghetti. When cooked, they turn translucent and smooth textured, yet are very soft on the tongue.

1. Cut beef into thin bite size pieces. Cut green peppers lengthwise into quarters. Slice onion and green onion (diagonally) thinly. Cut chrysanthemum leaves and mushrooms into bite size pieces.

2. In a saucepan add beef stock, beef, onion and green onion. Cook until onion is cooked. Add **A** and bring to a boil; add green peppers and mushrooms.

3. Pour in beaten egg using a whirling motion. Cook noodles and rinse quickly under running water; drain. Just before serving, blanch in boiling water and drain. In serving bowl place noodles and pour soup over. Garnish with chrysanthemum leaves. Sprinkle with finely chopped green onion and pepper, if desired.

COLD NOODLES WITH HOT SAUCE 비빔면 *(Bibimmyeon)* **Noodles**

INGREDIENTS: 4 servings

14 oz (400g) dried Korean noodles
Sauce
- 1¾ oz (50g) KOCHU JANG (hot sauce–See P95)
- 1 oz (30g) green onion, minced
- 3 T marinade liquid of CHINESE CABBAGE KIMCHEE (See P80)
- 2 T each sugar and vinegar
- 1 T each soy sauce and sesame oil
- 1 T soy seasoned ground meat (below)
- 1 T roasted sesame seeds
- ½ t ground chili pepper
- ½ t crushed garlic
- MSG

2 oz (60g) braised beef (**COUNTRY STYLE BEEF**–See P12)
Seasoned cucumber and *daikon* radish (See P72)
2 eggs, hard boiled
Roasted *nori* seaweed

Adding liquid marinade from KIMCHEE makes this a hot dish.

Soy Seasoned Ground Meat (1–2)
1. In a saucepan add 5 cups water and 18 oz (500g) each ground pork and beef, cook and stir to crumble meat.

2. Skim off residue carefully. Stir in 5 T each soy sauce and sugar, 5 t *mirin* and 2½ t crushed garlic; simmer until the sauce has evaporated.

3. Combine sauce ingredients.

4. Cook noodles, rinse under running water, drain (See P 73). Just before serving blanch in boiling water; drain.

5. Add noodles to (3), blend well so the noodles absorb the sauce.

6. In a serving bowl, place seasoned noodles, top with braised beef slices, seasoned vegetable, egg slices. Garnish with shredded *nori* seaweed, if desired.

STEAMED BUNS 만두 *(Mandu)*

A variety of fillings are wrapped in pasta.

Pasta
- 7 oz (200g) all-purpose flour
- ⅔ cup water
- 1 egg yolk
- Salad oil
- Pinch of salt

Filling
- 3½ oz (100g) each ground pork and beef
- 7 oz (200g) firm *tofu*
- 5¼ oz (150g) CHINESE CABBAGE KIMCHEE (See P80)
- 1¾ oz (50g) green onions
- 1 T flour
- ½ whole egg
- Crushed garlic
- Roasted sesame seeds
- Pepper

Cornstarch for flouring
YANG NYEOM JANG (See P95)

*****Serving As Soup:** Heat beef stock to boiling point, season with salt, pepper, and crushed garlic. Add buns, heat to boiling.

Making Pasta (1–6)
1. In a bowl place flour and egg yolk.

2. Dropping water little by little, knead well. Add salad oil and salt, knead again.

3. Work into a ball. Seal in plastic wrap, let stand 30 minutes.

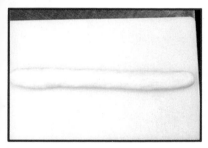

4. Shape into a 1 in (2.5cm) diam cylinder.

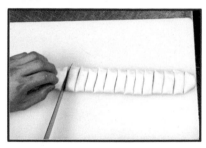

5. Cut into 20 slices, ½ in (1.5cm) wide.

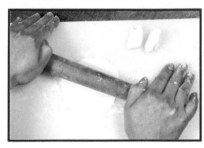

6. Lightly flour the dough, roll out into 3 in (8cm) diam circles.

Making Filling (7–9)
7. Rinse KIMCHEE, drain and chop finely.

8. Drain *tofu* (See P 60). Chop green onion finely.

9. In a bowl put all filling ingredients, mix thoroughly by hand until smooth.

10. Place 1 T filling onto each sheet of pasta.

11. Moisten the edges of sheet, over-wrap the half with the other half; seal tightly.

12. Put the ends together, moistening the joint.

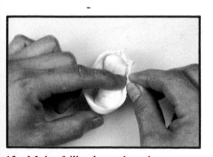

13. Make frills along the edge.

14. Steam in a hot steamer over high heat 7–8 minutes. Serve immediately with YANG NYEOM JANG.

SHRIMP AND VEGETABLE WRAP-UPS 밀쌈 (*Milsam*)

"Sam" refer to wrapping ingredients.

INGREDIENTS: 4 servings

Wrappers

- 1½ cups all-purpose flour
- 1½ cups water
- 1 egg yolk
- ¼ T salt

4 oz (115g) shelled shrimp
4 dried *shiitake* mushrooms
1 small cucumber
Salad oil
Sesame oil
Roasted sesame seeds
Salt and white pepper

Sauce

- 3 T soy sauce
- 1 T vinegar
- 1 t sugar
- Shredded lemon rind
- MSG

½ lemon cup

* MILSAM is a common version of the Korean Royal recipe, KUJE-OLPAN. KUJEOLPAN is served in a special octagonal lacquer ware box which is divided into 9 sections, holding 8 kinds of fillings and wrappers. In formal occasions, 5 colors — red, white, blue, yellow and black — are assorted so that matching color comes from opposite section. To serve at home, prepare several fillings using everyday ingredients and serve on a platter.
* Freeze wrappers for later use. Thaw at room temperature.
* It is important to cook and stir ingredients over very high heat to keep moisture in. Do not overcook.
* When making lemon cup, cut a thin slice from bottom of the lemon so it sits flat. Shred the slice finely for sauce.

Making Wrappers (1–5)
1. In a bowl, place flour, egg yolk, and salt.

2. Dropping water little by little whisk vigorously until sticky; let stand 30 minutes.

3. Stain through a strainer, whisk again.

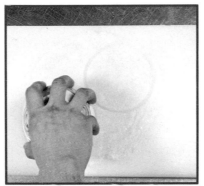

4. Lightly grease bottom of a skillet (wipe off excess oil). Gently pour in dough to form a paper-thin sheet. Cook over high heat, turning over when edges come apart.

5. Using edges of a bowl or dish, cut out cooked sheets into circles. Makes 20 wrappers.

6. Put shrimp in a colander, shake in salted water. Blanch in salted boiling water.

7. Drain shrimp, mix with roasted sesame seeds, sesame oil, salt and white pepper to taste.

8. Shred *shiitake* mushrooms, stir-fry in hot sesame oil, season with salt and pepper. Sprinkle with sesame seeds.

9. Halve cucumber lengthwise, cut into thin diagonal slices. Salt and squeeze. Cook and season as for mushrooms. Arrange wrappers and fillings on a platter. Combine sauce ingredients and serve in a lemon cup. Garnish with mustard, if desired.

KIMCHEE is Korea's most traditional condiment always served at every meal.

INGREDIENTS: 4 servings

3 heads Chinese cabbages (22¼ lbs, 10kg)

{ 14 oz (400g) salt (4% weight of cabbage)

21 oz (600g) *daikon* radish

{ ⅕ oz (6g) salt (1% weight of radish)

Marinade

A {
1⅓ cups *dashi* stock (See P93)
2 T flour
2 T salted opossum shrimp
2 T anchovy sauce

{
2 bunches chives (1¾ oz, 50g), cut into 1½ in (4cm) length

B {
7 oz (200g) finely chopped green onion
5¼ oz (150g) ground chili pepper
3½ oz (100g) sugar
1¾ oz (50g) grated ginger root
2 T crushed garlic
MSG or *dashi-no-moto* (instant stock —See P94)

* Success of KIMCHEE depends on the salting process. Temperature, weight, and pickling time are the important elements.

1. Discard dead outer leaves. Cut in half.

2. Make a slit at root end, pull apart each half. If using small Chinese cabbage, cut in half.

3. Sprinkle salt between leaves, heavily over root side.

4. In a large container, place (3), top with a light weight and let stand a whole day and night (in summertime, overnight), turning over several times for even salting. Rinse in water; drain and set aside 30 minutes. Peel *daikon* radish, shred and sprinkle with salt; squeeze out water gently.

5. Prepare marinade. In a small pan heat **A** ingredients to boiling, constantly stirring.

6. Reduce heat to medium. Continue to cook stirring constantly to prevent burning. When forming a paste, remove from heat; cool. When completely cooled, add **B** and radish, mix.

place. Moisture comes out in 2–3 days, but do not take out at this point. Leave a further 4–5 days (shown above) at least. Take out necessary amount, press down remainder to remove air.

7. Between leaves, spread marinade paste. Grease your hand with sesame oil to prevent irritation caused by the chili pepper.

8. Folding each section in two, pack in rectangular container. Cover with plastic wrap, keep in cold and dark

KIMCHEE

KIMCHEE, this moist Korean pickle is now tempting the world's appetite with its subtle heat and sourness.

In ancient time and still now Korean winters are long and severe. The harsh conditions forced people to preserve vegetables for this season. The word KIMCHEE in Korean means "sunken vegetable", Chinese cabbages and *daikon* radishes were "sunk" into salted water and seasonings added, such as chili pepper, and later the special flavor of salted fish. Thus KIMCHEE became the most gorgeous and colorful of all pickles.

KIMCHEE can be called fermented vegetables, since many kinds of bacterial reactions contribute to build its flavor.
Most important is lactic acid which aids digestion.

The pungent action of the chili peppers, capsaicin stimulates the mucous membranes of the stomach. Organic acids control stomach secretions and fermentation produces vitamin B1, B2, B12 and nicotinic acid amides, etc. Moreover, the vegetable fibers also activate bowel movement, solving constipation.

KIMCHEE is always on the Korean dining table no matter how poor the meal is. It goes well with white rice, and is a good appetizer for drinks. It gives special flavor to stews and sautéed vegetables. Try it on noodles, rice, or make your own variations.

Just prior to winter, in November the Koreans take a "KIMCHEE HOLIDAY". Neighbors customarily cooperate in each other's yards for the preparation of KIMCHEE.

Quick & Easy KIMCHEE

Recently an instant KIMCHEE base has become readily available at oriental supermarkets. It is useful for those who do not want any failure with homemade KIMCHEE.

This is another form of vegetable pickles.

INGREDIENTS

1 *daikon* radish with leaves (about 2¼ lbs, 1 kg)

⅔ oz (20 g) salt (2% weight of radish)

Marinade

A ⎧ ⅔ cup *dashi* stock (See P94)
2 T flour
2 T salted opposum shrimp
2 T anchovy sauce

⎧ 1 bunch chives, cut into 1 in (2.5 cm)
7 oz (200 g) finely chopped green onions

B ⎧ 1¾ oz (50 g) grated ginger root
3 T ground chili pepper
2 T sugar
1½ T crushed garlic
MSG

★ Prepare marinade ahead as directed on P81 – **CHINESE CABBAGE KIMCHEE.**

* Originally this KIMCHEE was from a Royal menu. A high official who fled from Seuol recalled his highlight life by tasting this handmade KIMCHEE of *daikon* radish, which made the local people interested and in trying it themselves.

1. Peel *daikon* radish, cut into 1 in (2.5 cm) dices. Cut the leaves into 1 in (2.5 cm) length. Rub salt evenly, top with a light weight, and let stand 2–3 hours, occasionally stirring for even salting.

2. When radish is watery and soft, rinse in water; drain. Let stand 30 minutes– 1 hour.

3. In a bowl mix *daikon* radish and marinade thoroughly. Transfer to a container, seal tightly, and place in a dark location. Start serving after 2–3 days.

Traditionally, people in Korea start the meal with this KIMCHEE drink.

INGREDIENTS: Makes 8 cups

4 oz (115g) Chinese cabbage
2/3 oz (20g) *daikon* radish
1/4 apple or pear
1/3 oz (10g) carrot
1/2 small cucumber
1/2 white part of green onion
1/3 oz (10g) garlic
1/3 oz (10g) ginger root
Japanese parsley

A { 6 cups water
1 1/2 t salt
1 t sugar

Ground chili pepper
MSG
Chili pepper, shredded
Pine nuts
Salt

* This KIMCHEE can be called "KIM-CHEE in the bath"; Lightly salted *daikon* radish or Chinese cabbage are soaked in marinade plus water to accelerate fermentation. The soaking liquor is also consumed. For its lighter flavor it is served like a dessert or taken as a good remedy for hangover.

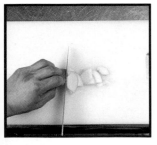

1. Finely shred or slice garlic.

2. Cut Chinese cabbage, *daikon* radish and cucumber into thin rectangles. Cut carrot into half-moons. Finely shred ginger root and green onion. Cut Japanese parsley into 1 in (2.5cm) length.

3. In a bowl place all vegetables but Japanese parsley. Sprinkle with salt, rub with hands. When soft, immediately rinse off salt.

4. In a container place (3). Combine **A** and pour over it. Let stand in cool place for half a day. Mix with shredded Japanese parsley and refrigerate. When serving, sprinkle with pine nuts and shredded chili pepper.

Chili-flavored *daikon* with a crispy texture.

4 oz (115g) dried *daikon* radish (See ∗)

A
- 1½ T soy sauce
- 1 t vinegar
- 1 t roasted sesame seeds
- ½ t ground chili pepper
- Crushed garlic

Sesame oil

∗ **Drying *daikon* radish:** Cut unpeeled *daikon* lengthwish into thin strips. Put on a large flat basket separated from each other, or hang in the air threading through strips. Dry under the sun 3–4 days, taking in during night-time to avoid dew. Occasionally turn over for even drying. When thoroughly dried, keep in plastic bags and air-tight container no more than 3 months. Freeze no more than 6 months.

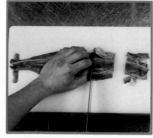

1. Soak dried *daikon* radish in large amount of water. Do not soak until soft as it spoils the crisp texture.

2. Rinse well, squeeze out water.

3. Cut into 2 in (5 cm) length. Thin soy sauce with adequate amount of water. Marinate *daikon* radish until it absorbs soy sauce flavor.

4. Just before serving, combine **A** in a bowl. Take out *daikon* radish and rub with **A**. Transfer to serving dish and sprinkle with sesame oil.

84

Garlic pickles are a fitting accompaniment to any Korean meal.

INGREDIENTS

15–18 bulbs garlic (2¼ lbs, 1 kg)
⅔ gal (2.5 lit) vinegar

A {
2½ cups soy sauce
2 cups water
3½ oz (100g) sugar
3 chili peppers, seeded
}

* The marinade can be used as a base of barbeque sauce or salad dressings.
* Separate and peel cloves of garlic, if you prefer.
* Leave 1 month before serving. Keep no more than 1 year.
* When serving, cut in half crosswise with skins still attached. Place cut side up, imitating flower petals.

1. Peel only outer skin of the garlic bulbs. Place in a container, pour over vinegar to cover. Put a weight on so garlics does not float. Leave 7–10 days.

2. In a saucepan bring **A** to boiling point, set aside to cool thoroughly. Discard vinegar of illustration #1, pour in sauce. Weight and leave in a shady place 1 month at least.

This unique Oriental green leaf can be eaten fresh or used as an aromatic garnish.

INGREDIENTS

7 oz (200g) green *shiso* leaves
2 cups water
1/5 cup salt (10% weight of water)
2 oz (60g) red *miso*
2 oz (60g) KOCHU JANG (hot sauce—
    See P95)
Roasted sesame seeds
Sesame oil

* Originally perilla leaves are used in place of green *shiso* leaves.

1. Clean green *shiso* leaves. Dissolve salt in water and add *shiso* leaves. Weight and leave 1 week.

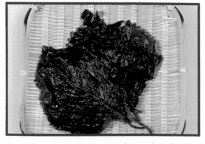

2. Take out leaves, rinse in fresh water; drain.

3. Blend red *miso* and KOCHU JANG (hot sauce) well. In a container with lid, place a layer of green *shiso* leaves, spread *miso* mixture using your fingers. Overlap another layer and repeat the process. Leave overnight. When serving, sprinkle with roasted sesame seeds and sesame oil, if desired.

This pungent relish goes with any dish.

INGREDIENTS

4 oz (115g) hot green peppers
2–3 cups water
Salt, 4% weight of water
4 oz (115g) red *miso*
Roasted sesame seeds
Sesame oil

* **Hot green pepper:** Immature hot red pepper (chili pepper), noted for strong flavor hot. Appears on the market in May and June.
* Red *miso* can be substituted by KOCHU JANG (hot sauce–See P 95).
* As this can be preserved for a pretty long period, it is recommended to pickle a large amount when in season. It is best when served after 2 weeks.

1. Remove stems of hot green peppers, rinse well; drain. Dissolve 4% salt into water, put peppers in, top with a weight and leave a week.

2. Rinse briefly in fresh water. In a container with a lid, place *miso* and peppers. Make sure peppers are not touching each other. Leave 2 weeks at least. When serving, wipe off *miso* lightly, place in a serving dish, and sprinkle with sesame oil.

Seafoods salted with spicy condiments create a delicious Korean taste.

INGREDIENTS

10¹/₂ oz (300g) small oysters
Salt, 5% weight of oysters
¹/₂ green onion, chopped finely
¹/₃ oz (10g) ginger root, shredded
4 T ground chili pepper
1 T crushed garlic
MSG

* Among many kinds of salted seafood in Korea, this is mostly admired. Be careful with the amount of salt for the smoothest touch.
* For even better flavor, add 1³/₄ oz (50g) shredded *daikon* radish or pears. In this case, do not store long.

1. Wash oysters in lightly salted water; drain. Sprinkle with salt to "shrink" the flesh.

2. Add remaining ingredients and mix well. Let stand overnight at least. Best in 2–3 days.

INGREDIENTS

7 oz (200g) shucked horse neck clams
1²/₅ oz (40g) salt
²/₃ oz (20g) ginger root

* Salting seafood for a long period accents seprate protein, thus improving the flavor and richness.
* Mix crushed garlic (2 cloves), if desired. It is also recommended to stir in sesame oil, ground chili pepper, roasted sesame seeds, vinegar or finely chopped green onion for a varied flavor.

1. Briefly wash clams; drain. Sprinkle with salt.

2. Add ginger juice and mix well. Put in a container and leave in dark, cool place, 10 days at least.

INFORMATION

BASIC TIPS

Garlic, sesame oil and **chili pepper** are three essential ingredients for Korean cooking. It is very important to buy quality products for your successful cooking.

Garilic can be stored in cool, dark place for sometime. Buy bulbs that are tightly closed, with unwrinkled skins of pinkish white to purple hue or white with purple streaks. For the best flavor finely chop or grate then crush (using garlic press or knife).

Sesame oil is made from sesame seeds which are rich in oil and protein, and a unique taste and aroma. Add to dish just before serving. Keep refrigerated after opening. Buy that which is made in the orient. Sesame oils from other origins are somewhat different.

Whole **chili peppers** keep fresh longer than ground. Generally in Korean cooking, chopped, coarse ground or finely ground chili peppers are used for cooking and finely shredded for garnishes. Store them in a tightly closed containers and keep them in a cool, dark place.

Before you attempt to cook, here are some steps for the best result.

1. **Read recipes carefully and thoroughly.**

2. **Before purchasing write down all neccessary ingredients.**

3. **Check all cooking equipment and place within reach.**

4. **Arrange all neccessary kitchen seasonings, spices and herbs within easy reach.**

5. **Prepare measuring cups, spoons and scales.**

6. **Prepare all serving bowls, plates and platters near you. You may need to keep some serving platters warm.**

7. **Prepare plenty of kitchen towels and/or paper towels.**

8. **While cooking, taste food as often as you wish. Under seasoning is better than over seasoning.**

PREPARATION

★ Basic Cutting Methods

When preparing ingredients use a sharp knife. Cut to bite size pieces making them easy to cook, eat and digest.

For decorative cuts, use the tip of knife. For peeling use the lower part of blade. The part from the center towards the tip is used for most cutting work.

Rounds

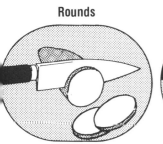

Round ingredients such as *daikon* radish or carrot are cut into the same thickness.

Diagonal Slices

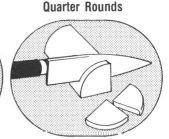

Thin round ingredients such as cucumber are sliced diagonally giving a large effect.

"Paring" Thin Fillets

Soft or fragile ingredients are placed flat and pared off with the knife parallel to the cutting board.

Quarter Rounds

Large round ingredients such as turnip or *daikon* radish are split into quarters and then sliced.

Half-rounds

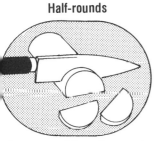

Large round ingredients such as *daikon* radish are split into halves and sliced

Wedges

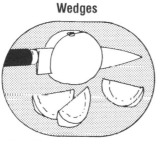

Ingredients such as lemon or onion are split into quarters then eighths.

Rolling Wedges

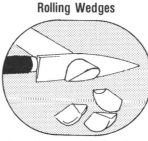

Ingredients are rolled and cut diagonally to give more sides for seasoning.

Rectangles

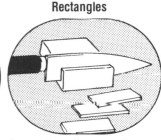

Large ingredients such as *daikon* radish are cut into 2 in (5cm) length and then sliced into ½ in (1.5cm) thickness.

Shreds

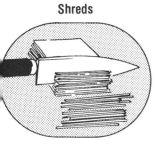

Ingredients are sliced into thin rectangles of 2–2½ in (5–6.5cm) length, layered and cut into thin matchlike sticks parallel to the fibers.

Sticks

Ingredients such as potato, carrot or bamboo shoot are cut into 2–2½ in (5–6.5cm) long, ⅜ in (1cm) wide sticks.

Dices

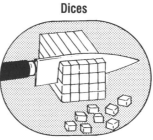

Ingredients are cut into ⅜ in (1cm) wide sticks, and then into ⅜ in (1cm) cubes.

Mincing

Shredded ingredients such as ginger root or green onion are chopped finely.

★ Rice Cooking

There are two types of rice available; white short-grain rice and white long-grain rice. Use white short-grain rice for Korean dishes. The short-grain rice is somewhat stickier and moister than long-grain rice. In the U.S., short-grain rice is grown extensively in California. Newly cropped rice needs less water and slightly shorter cooking time than old rice. A little practice is needed to make perfect rice, however if you cook a lot of rice, an automatic rice cooker will make your work a lot easier, so it's a good investment.

Following is a key to shiny and fluffy rice. Go ahead with these basic tips for successful rice cooking. It's easy.

1. Measure rice carefully.

2. Wash rice in a big bowl of water. Rub grains gently, wet grains break easily.

3. Remove any bran or polishing agent. Drain off water well. Repeat this step until water is almost clear.

4. To make a fluffy and moister rice, set rice aside for at least 30 minutes in summer and one hour in winter. This allows ample time for rice to absorb the water.

5. In cooking pot, add rice and correct amount of water. Cover with lid.

Rice increases in volume as it cooks, twice to three times, depending on the kind of rice you use.

COOKED RICE	RICE	WATER
2$\frac{1}{2}$ cups	1 cup	1$\frac{1}{4}$ cups
5 cups	2 cups	2$\frac{1}{2}$ cups
7$\frac{1}{2}$ cups	3 cups	3$\frac{3}{4}$ cups
10 cups	4 cups	5 cups

PREPARATION

[How to Cook]

- **MEDIUM HEAT UNTIL WATER BOILS**
Cook rice over medium heat until water boils. Do not bring it to boiling point quickly. If the quantity of rice is large, cook rice over high heat from the beginning. The heat can be carried into the center of rice if cooked over medium heat.

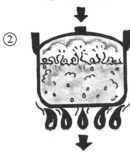

- **HIGH HEAT FOR 1 MINUTE AFTER BOILING**
When it begins to boil, turn heat to high and cook for 1 minute. Never lift lid while cooking. Since the lid might bounce from the pressure of the steam, it is better to place a weight, or some dishes on the lid. Rice absorbs enough water.

- **TURN HEAT TO LOW FOR 4–5 MINUTES**
Turn heat to low and cook for 4-5 minutes (Be careful not to overboil). Then the pot begins to steam.

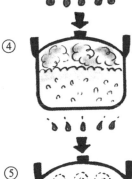

- **THE LOWEST HEAT FOR 10 MINUTES**
Reduce heat to the lowest for 10 minutes. Every grain of rice absorbs water and becomes plump. It is liable to burn, so cook over the lowest heat.

- **TURN OFF AND LET STAND FOR 10 MINUTES**
Turn off the heat and let rice stand, covered for 10 minutes. During this 10 minutes the grains are allowed to "settle", and the cooking process is completed by the heat retained in the rice and the walls of the pot.

●**AUTOMATIC RICE COOKER**
Today rice is cooked daily in many household in an automatic electric or gas rice cooker. The automatic rice cooker, an appliance developed in the postwar period, cooks perfect rice. Put washed rice in the cooker, add water. There are measurment marks in the cooker for water and rice volume. Then cover and turn on. Automatic controls take over cooking, reducing heat at exact time, and also in some models, the rice is kept warm till needed. Cookers come in various sizes, from tiny ones holding only a few cups to large ones used in restaurants. Automatic rice cookers, either electric or gas can be obtained at oriental stores.

PREPARATION

★How to Make Stocks

A) Beef Stock

Beef tendons make the best Korean soup stock, but if not available, use any left-over bits in the refrigerator.

INGREDIENTS: Makes approx 3 quarts (3 lit)
21 oz (600g) beef tendons or shank
1 gal (4 lit) water
3½ oz (100g) ginger root
3 oz (85g) garlic
3½ oz (100g) green onions
DIRECTIONS
1. In a saucepan put all ingredients and cook over high heat.
2. When the liquid is almost boiling, skim and reduce heat. Simmer for 3 hours. Continue to skim.
3. Strain through a cloth, heat to just before boiling point; remove from heat. When completely cooled, transfer to non-metalic container and keep refrigerated. It can be stored a week in the refrigerator.
QUICK & EASY METHOD
Dissolve stock cubes in boiling water.

B) Chicken Stock

INGREDIENTS: Makes approx 3 quarts (3 lit)
21 oz (600g) chicken bones or thigh
1 gal (4 lit) water
3½ oz (100g) ginger root
3 oz (85g) garlic
3½ oz (100g) green onions
DIRECTIONS
1. Rinse chicken bones in water; crack or cut into pieces.
2. In a saucepan put all ingredients and cook over high heat. When liquid is boiling, reduce heat and simmer for 3 hours, skimming constantly.

3 Strain through a cloth, heat to boiling point; immediately remove from heat. When completely cooled, transfer to non-metallic container and keep refrigerated.

C) *Dashi* Stock (dried sardine stock)

***Dashi* stock is used not only in soups but also as a base of each dish.**

For dried sardine stock, choose well-dried, middle-sized sardines. Avoid sardines which are oxidized, have no heads or bellies, or have yellow bellies.

INGREDIENTS: Makes 4 cups
1²/₅ oz (40g) dried sardines
4 cups water
DIRECTIONS
1. Discard heads and intestines from sardines. Tear into small pieces.
2. In a saucepan, put sardines and water, cook uncovered over medium heat.
3. Skim. Just before the boiling point, reduce heat and cook 10 minutes.
4. In a bowl or a pan, lay wet cloth (muslin). Pour stock over and squeeze out the liquid.
QUICK & EASY METHOD
Today many kinds of instant *dashi* mix are in the market — powdered, granulated and concentrated types are available. Whatever the kind ¹/₆ oz (5g) instant *dashi* mix yields about 2½ cups *dashi* stock. If not available, substitute with stock cubes although the flavor is different.

★How to Make Shredded Omelet

Shredded omelet is often used in Korean dishes in order to accentuate the color. Sometimes the egg yolks and egg whites are cooked separately to add two-tone (yellow & white) colors. Do not brown the surface when cooking.

1. Beat 1 egg lightly (do not whisk), add a pinch of salt. Pour into hot thinly greased skillet or square omelet pan.

2. Roll the skillet round to spread evenly, over very low heat. When the surface is nearly dry, separate the edges and turn over; cook slightly.

3. Cut into 1–1½ in (2.5–4cm) width and place in layers.

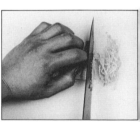

4. Shred finely. 1 egg yields 3 T (1²/₅ oz, 40g) shredded omelet.

PREPARATION

★ How to Make KOCHU JANG (Hot Sauce)

INGREDIENTS
7½ cups glutenous rice powder
5½ cups chili powder
5½ cups salt
4 cups YEODKIREUM powder (dried barley sprout malt)
2 cups MEJU powder (soy bean malt)*
8⅓ cups (2 lit) water

*Steamed soy beans are made into dumplings, fermented, dried, and then powdered. Available in Korean markets.

DIRECTIONS
1. In a bowl, combine YEODKIREUM powder and water. Mix well using fingers; strain.
2. In a large pan, gently pour the top liquid of 1. Add glutenous rice powder, mix well, heat slowly until 113°F (45°C); remove from heat and let stand until the rice powder dissolves.
3. Heat to boiling, reduce heat and boil down 30 minutes.
4. Transfer to a large bowl, allow to cool. When completely cooled, mix in MEJU powder and stir well.
5. Add chili powder to the bowl and blend well; leave overnight.
6. Pour in 4 cups salt and mix well. Transfer to a large container, sprinkle with remaining 1½ cups salt to cover the surface. Cover with a gauge and leave in sunny place to accelerate fermentation. Occasionally stir when bubbles rise for 1 month.

*When transferring to container, do not fill it for fermented liquid may overflow.
*During fermentation, cover the container at night.

KOCHU JANG has made many contributions to Korean cookery with its zesty flavor. It gives flavor and at the same time draws flavor from the ingredients. No one-pot dish, rice dishes, salads or stews are Korean without this sauce.

Each Korean family owns its recipe, but the common method is the "slow and steady" maturation to form a good harmony of hot, sweet and sour flavors. Born from the severe weather and environment, KOCHU JANG became the Korean's masterpiece of seasonings.

Make a large amount and store as it keeps well. When buying commercial products, it is better to taste first for as they all differ.

★ How to Make YANG NYEOM JANG

The Korean "YANG NYEOM" stands for condiments, including seasonings and spices. On the other hand the word "JANG" is found in seasonings such a KAN JANG (soy sauce), TOEN JANG (*miso*, soy bean paste), or KOCHU JANG (hot sauce), meaning fermented sauce as you can see.

This JANG is blended with sesame oil, garlic, scallion, pepper, sesame seeds, and so on, to make YANG NYEOM JANG as you guessed. Here are two typical kinds of YANG NYEOM JANG recipes. Master these basic recipes, then try your own blend. Matching dishes are given on the right-hand side.

——— Type A ———

INGREDIENTS
3 T soy sauce
⅓ oz (10g) hot green pepper, minced
1 T minced green onion
1 t crushed garlic
1 t ground chili pepper
1 t roasted sesame seeds
1 t sesame oil
Pepper
MSG

MATCHING DISHES
BROILED FISH (P 39)
GRUEL RICE WITH VEGETABLES (P 66)
RICE WITH SOYBEAN SPROUTS (P 68)
HOT NOODLE DISH (P 74)
STEAMED BUNS (P 76)

——— Type B ———

INGREDIENTS
2 T soy sauce
2 T vinegar
2 t chopped pine nuts
Chopped chives
Lemon juice

MATCHING DISHES
STEAMED TONGUE (P 29)
STEAMED FISH (P 38)
STUFFED CABBAGE ROLLS (P 54)
SEAFOOD AND VEGETABLE OMELET (P 56)
SHRIMP AND VEGETABLE WRAP-UPS (P 78)

COOKING METHODS

Soups
국 (KUK)·탕 (TANG)

KUK and TANG both mean soup. Korean meals are always accompanied by a bowl of KUK or TANG. There are lots of variations including the bases of soy sauce, salt and *miso*.

A) Beef Soups
Beef tendons, shanks or knuckles are simmered with garlic and green onions, and simply seasoned to taste with salt or soy sauce. Served with condiments like minced green onion, crushed garlic, sprinkled with pepper.

B) Seafood Soups
Depending on the flavor extracted from the seafood, soy sauce or *miso* is added. Suitable garnishes are coriander, chrysanthemum leaves or green onion.

C) Vegetable Soups
Not only cultivated vegetables but edible mountain plants are used to make flavorful soups. Some vegetables are added to the stock uncooked while some are parboiled or seasoned with *miso* or KOCHU JANG (hot sauce–See P 95).

Meat/Seafood Au Naturel
회 (HWE)

HWE is any fresh slices of meat or seafood, dipped in special sauce and eaten.

A) SENGHWE
Very fresh meat or seafood is sprinkled with *sake* to get rid of the odor. A popular dip is a mixture of KOCHU JANG (hot sauce–See P 95), vinegar, lemon juice and ginger juice. YUKWE (SEASONED RAW BEEF–See P 25) is shredded fresh beef dressed with a spicy sauce which should be accompanied by pear juice or shreds.

B) SUKHWE
Fresh meat or seafood is grilled lightly to make "frost". Sometimes it is dusted with cornstarch and blanched in boiling water to "frost". When blanching seafood, dash of *sake* or white wine is added to the water. The meat should not be heated through. The dipping sauce varies from CHO KOCHU JANG (hot and sour sauce) to many kinds of YANG NYEOM JANG based on soy sauce.

One-Pot Dishes
찌개 (CHIGHE)·전골 (CHONGOL)

Korean one-pot dishes have two types:

A) CHIGHE
Seafoods, meats, vegetables, *tofu* and mushrooms are cooked in *miso*, KOCHU JANG (hot sauce–See P 95), soy sauce and salted fish. This little salty dish makes a popular everyday meal to go with white rice. CHIGHE with *tofu* or KIMCHEE is an easy and economical dish.

B) CHONGOL
A gorgeous assortment of seasonal seafood, meats and vegetables in one-pot. Ingredients are cooked in the previously described Cheon process see page 56.

CHONGOL originated from the Royal Court, now served on entertaining and celebrating occasions. All ingredients are cut to fit the size of pot, and beautifully arranged.

"Royal Hot Pot (SINSEON–LO) is a typical example of CHONGOL featuring CHEON (egg batter coated food) and ginkgo nuts, pine nuts, walnuts, etc.

COOKING METHODS

Salads
무침 (MUCHIM)

MUCHIM is a general term for dressed vegetables, including NAMOOL (See P44). NAMOOL originally meant edible plants, which were eaten as cold or hot salads, hence the name.

A) SENGCHE
Cleaned vegetables are cut into bite size pieces and dressed with vinegared soy sauce, vinegared-KOCHU JANG, or mustard. Chili pepper is added before seasoning with salt, if necessary. Sweet seasoning (sugar) enhances the whole flavor.

B) SUKCHE
Vegetables are cooked in various ways—boiled, stir-fried, or steamed—then dressed. Besides a good choice of fresh vegetables and preparation, blending of the seasonings such as sesame seeds, sesame oil and garlic is most important.

When using strong-flavored vegetable, sesame oil is used to coat and then chili pepper is added.

The other MUCHIM is called CHAPCHE, stir-fried vegetable shreds. Several kinds of vegetables are cut into fine julienne strips and sautéed individually until adequately tender. When mixed, they make a crisp and delicious salad.

Simmered Food
조림 (CHORIM)

CHORIM means to season various ingredients and simmer until tender. Seafoods, meats and root vegetables are used.

The point in simmering is to choose the process to fit each ingredient. Some vegetables with harsh tastes should be prepared by blanching in hot or cold water, salting or deep-frying. Another point is to cut ingredients into the same size and cook tougher foods first. This enables the taste to penetrate evenly.

To season, soy sauce is used as a base, and *sake,* sugar, garlic, ginger root, green onion, sesame oil or KOCHU JANG (hot sauce-See P95) are added. The order of adding seasonings is also an important element. Seasonings like sugar which take a longer time to penetrate into food should be added first, and strong flavored seasonings like sesame oil must come last.

After the boiling point, the heat must be lowered, and the residue removed from the top.

Stir-fried Food
볶음 (POKKUM)

POKKUM stands for sautéed dishes. Soy sauce, *miso* or salt is used to season ingredients which are then fried in sesame oil. For a richer taste, crushed garlic, sesame seeds and chili pepper may be added.

It is important to stir-fry quickly over very high heat, and to add tough ingredients first. Combine all the seasonings beforehand.

COOKING METHODS

Egg Batter Coated Food
전 (CHEON)

Meats, white fish, vegetables which can be fried are the ingredients for CHEON. They are cut into bite size pieces, seasoned to taste with salt and pepper, coated with flour, then with beaten eggs.

A griddle is an ideal utensil for this method. Ingredients are pressed down so the excess moisture escapes, and the aroma is kept in.

An intricate method, but the gentle tasting batter emphasizes the inner flavor with its vivid yellow color. CHEON is a must on Korean ceremony tables as a traditional entertainment.

CHEON is served hot, accompanied with vinegar and soy sauce.

It is interesting to know that no hot peppers are used in this method.

Grilled Food
구이 (KUEE)·적 (JEOK)

Korean grilling methods are divided into two:

A) KUEE
Meats, seafoods and vegetables are grilled. Whatever the ingredients, they must be cooked (not stir-fried) over high heat, on well-preheated grills.

B) JEOK
Korean Shish Kebabs are of three types:

Type I — Ingredients are marinated, grilled with spicy sauce basted on and pine nuts used to garnish.

Type II — Marinated ingredients are grilled, cut to the same length and skewered, then grilled again.

Type III — Ingredients are skewered, dusted with flour, coated with beaten egg, and fried (See P 57-KEBAB KOREAN STYLE). Served with vinegar and soy sauce.

Steamed Food
찜 (CHIM)

CHIM includes steaming in bamboo steamer, boiling, and simmering. Joints of meat are cooked in this method to tenderize and retain shape. It also keeps the aroma and nutritional value inside. Garnished with shredded omelet, shredded chili pepper and pine nuts, this is an essential dish on ceremonial occasions in Korea.

COOKING METHODS

Rice
밥 (BAP)

While a bowl of plain rice always accompanies Korean dishes, one-meal rice dishes are called BAP. Barley, Italian (Foxtail) millet, or corn is sometimes mixed with rice. Follwing are examples of BAP cooking.

A) Pilaf
Rice is steamed with KIMCHEE, soybean sprouts, fresh oysters or clams, in soup stock. Served with favorite YANG NYEOM JANG.

B) BIBIMBAP
BIBIM means to mix, BAP means rice. On top of hot white rice, many ingredients such as assorted vegetables, stir-fried beef, seasoned raw beef, and shredded omelet are arranged. They are all mixed with sesame oil or KOCHU JANG (hot sauce–See P95) when eating. BIBIMBAP in KYONGJU district is well known as for this local specialty.

C) KUKBAP
Hot soup is poured over hot white rice and immediately served.

D) YAKBAP
Glutinous rice is steamed with chestnuts, dates, ginkgo nuts, pine nuts and raisins, and then mixed with honcy, cinnamon, soy sauce and sesame oil, and steamed again. YAK means medicine. Here you can see the Korean principle "Food is a medicine". The word YAK appears in many dishes using precious ingredients. It is served on party occasions including New Year holiday and birthdays.

Noodles
면 (MYEON)

For the Korean the length of noodles are a symbol of longevity. Noodles are a must on celebrating tables such as birthdays (especially 60th birthdays) and weddings.

The main ingredients are buckwheat flour, flour, potato starch, and corn flour, depending on the district. There are hand-made noodles and machine-made noodles and machine-made thin noodles or even finger-thick noodles.

There are also various cooking methods; cold noodles in cold soup is a popular summer treat, and BIBIMMYEON (COLD NOODLES WITH HOT SAUCE–See P75) has a gorgeous assortment of vegetable and meats and served with hot sauce.

Available in Korean or Oriental markets.

Pickles
김치 (KIMCHEE) · 장아찌 (CHANG–A–CHEE)

Out of all Korean pickles KIMCHEE is the most typical one with over a hundred variations. It is now loved around the world. The complex flavor created by fermentation is based on successful salting process; the temperature, weight, amount of salt and salting time affect one another, and gives a subtle balance.

KIMCHEE adds a special accent to one-pot dishes, sautéed dishes, and salads.

Another popular pickle is called CHANG–A–CHEE. It is a preserve pickled in soy sauce, *miso*, KOCHU JANG (hot sauce–See P95), etc.

MENU PLANNING

Traditionally the most important meal of the day is considered to be breakfast, and lunch is less important than breakfast and dinner. Generally noodles or gruel rice dishes garnished with KIMCHEE are served at lunch time, usually accompanied by fruit and rice cakes.

Today many households in Korea serve Western style breakfast, yet for special occasions such as a birthday, people invite friends and guests to breakfast. They prepare many special dishes for the occasion. Also there are special dates to celebrate on each month of the year and people seem to enjoy seasonal ingredients and dishes. These ceremonial dates are based on the old lunar calender. A Korean banquet is a very elaborate affair usually for a large group. The emphasis of the recipes in this book is on informal everyday meals, so apart from traditional customs. You may plan and prepare your menu easily, leaving time to enjoy your company, rather than being stuck in the kitchen. Generally rice, KIMCHEE and soup always accompany a meal.

The following chart illustrates types of cooking methods and the number of side dishes to be served.

NUMBER OF SIDE DISHES \ COOKING METHODS	*ONE-POT DISHES	VEGETABLES		GRILLED FOOD	SIMMERED FOOD	EGG BATTER COATED FOOD	DRIED FOOD	MEAT/ SEAFOOD AU NATUREL
		COOKED	RAW					
3		O	O	O				
5	O	O	O	O		O	O	
7	O	O	O	O	O	O	O	O
9	O	O	2 dishes	2 dishes	O	O	O	O
12	O	2 dishes	2 dishes	2 dishes	O	2 dishes	O	2 dishes

* One-pot dish is not included in the number of side dishes.

Nine or twelve dishes are generally served for festivals, ceremonies or royal family as the cuisine of the royal court.

MENU PLANNING

Introduced here are several ideas for menus classified by seasons and the number of diners. You might think there are too many dishes, but serve smaller portions than directed in each recipe. Or choose one or two dishes as the main, and serve smaller portions for the rest.

Use these combinations for entertaining or at family dinners.

for Two

Summer	Winter
COLD CUCUMBER SOUP (P 19)	CHICKEN SOUP (P 18)
SEAFOOD SALAD (P 43)	MIXED VEGETABLES WITH SEAFOOD (P 47)
STEAMED SMALL GREEN PEPPERS (P 51)	SEASONED RAW BEEF (P 25)
TOASTED *NORI* SEAWEED (P 13)	TOASTED *NORI* SEAWEED (P 13)
BARBECUED MEAT (P 20)	*TOFU* STEAK (P 60)
LEAF ROLLS (P 11)	BARBECUED MEAT (P 20)
DAIKON RADISH KIMCHEE (P 82)	LEAF ROLLS (P 11)
COLD NOODLE DISH (P 72)	CHINESE CABBAGE KIMCHEE (P 80)
	COOKED RICE IN HOT BROTH (P 65)

for Three to Four

Summer	Winter
ROLLED HAM (P 10)	SHRIMP AND VEGETABLE WRAP-UPS (P 78)
CLAMS AND *WAKAME* SEAWEED (P 42)	MIXED VEGETABLES WITH BEEF (P 46)
COUNTRY STYLE BEEF (P 12)	STEAMED CLAMS (P 41)
STIR-FRIED GARLIC STALKS (P 49)	SEAFOOD AND VEGETABLE OMELET (P 56)
STUFFED CABBAGE ROLLS (P 54)	STUFFED CABBAGE ROLLS (P 54)
SKEWERED BEEF AND VEGETABLES (P 24)	BRAISED SHORT RIBS WITH VEGETABLES (P 28)
COLD KIMCHEE DRINKS (P 83)	STIR-FRIED PORK WITH KIMCHEE (P 30)
TOFU CASSEROLE WITH *MISO* (P 63)	BOUILLABAISSE–KOREAN STYLE (P 34)
VEGETABLES AND BEEF ON RICE (P 64)	COOKED RICE (P 92)
	DAIKON RADISH KIMCHEE (P 82)

for Eight or More

Summer	Winter
ROLLED HAM (P 10)	ROLLED HAM (P 10)
SHRIMP AND VEGETABLE WRAP-UPS (P 78)	SHRIMP AND VEGETABLE WRAP-UPS (P 78)
SEAFOOD SALAD (P 43)	MIXED VEGETABLES WITH SEAFOOD (P 47)
SEAFOOD AND VEGETABLE OMELET (P 56)	ROLLED-EGG-OMELET (P 58)
WHITE FISH SALAD (P 33)	STEAMED TONGUE (P 29)
STEAMED EGG CUSTARD (P 59)	FRESH FISH WITH HOT SAUCE (P 32)
OVEN-BARBECUED SPARERIBS (P 23)	*TOFU* HOT POT (P 62)
ROLLED RICE WITH *NORI* SEAWEED (P 70)	BARBECUED MEAT (P 20)
GARLIC PICKLES (P 85)	LEAF ROLLS (P 11)
CHINESE CABBAGE KIMCHEE (P 80)	COLD KIMCHEE DRINKS (P 83)
DAIKON RADISH KIMCHEE (P 82)	SALTED OYSTERS (P 88)
GRUEL RICE WITH VEGETABLES (P 66)	CHINESE CABBAGE KIMCHEE (P 80)
	VEGETABLE SOUP (P 16)
	RICE WITH SOYBEAN SPROUTS (P 68)

[I] Korean Tables

Brief History of Korean Food

It is said, "History of culinary art represents the history of the people." What is called Korean cuisine today has developed along with the people's history. After the Yi Dynasty, characteristics from each area and class mingled with each other and have been handed down till now.

In other words people have blended their local specialties and royal family's cuisine into their own dishes.

One feature of the Korean table was that all the courses were served at one time. Especially at seasonal events or entertaining occasions, the table was filled with all sorts of delicacies, desserts and wine bottles, which have been expressed in a saying "So abundant and florid that the legs of the table weighed down!"

However as simplicity spread abroad this extravagant style diminished, and people nowadays tend to take one course meals.

Food Is a Medicine

The Koreans maintain the idea of "Food is a medicine" that is, when there is any disorder, the first thing they do is not to take medicine but take revitalizing food.

For this reason they created many tonic dishes such as SANGYETANG—chicken soup with ginseng and beef liver au naturel.

The Koreans try to take as many herbs as possible in their daily life. Balloonflower root is eaten for soothing coughs, pine nuts for longevity, and so on.

Ingredients and Cooking Methods

Usually the ingredients are not used alone but mixed with others. They are cooked partially in order to leave their natural flavors.

A good example can be BIBIMBAP (See P 64), which has different vegetables and meat seasoned differently and assorted on rice. The Koreans mix everything together when eating and enjoy distinguishing each ingredient in the mouth.

Korean dishes are not Korean without KAJUN YANG NYEOM, combined seasonings (KAJUN means many, YANG NYEOM means seasonings and condiments). How you mix the salt, *miso*, and soy sauce with chili pepper and sesame oil, etc. decides the success of Korean cookery.

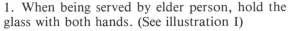

FACETS OF KOREAN CULTURE

[II] Drinking and Party Etiquette

The Koreans enjoy drinking as much as anybody else in the world. And such alcoholic expressions as "Can't carry that much on one's back but in one's stomach!" may be often heard.

Popular drinks are McKOLRY, CHONGJONG, SOJU, *sake*, BUPJU to name a few. Other wines such as ginseng or garlic are taken for the sake of stamina. Besides individual homes have a good stock of fruit wine just as in any other country. From these variety of wines, the most adequate is chosen for the day's meal.

Etiquette on drinking occasions include several "strict laws" as you can imagine from Eastern politeness. Remember the following points when drinking with elder person(s).

1. When being served by elder person, hold the glass with both hands. (See illustration I)
2. When actually drinking, slightly turning your face and drink slowly. (See illustration II)
3. When returning the glass to the elder person, hold it in your right hand, with your left hand supporting the right elbow gently. (See illustration III)
4. When pouring, hold the bottle in your right hand, with your left hand supporting the right elbow gently, then pour carefully. (See illustration IV)

Relax yourself when drinking with your colleagues, friends or family. One special note may be that when inviting guests to a private house, females never serve alcohol even if they are the wife or daughter. This custom possibly came from the long history of discriminating the professional hostesses.

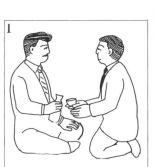
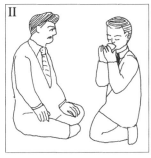
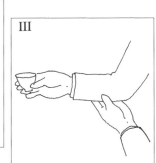
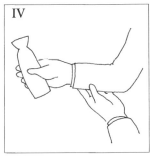

[III] Refreshments and Cakes

In the early days when Korea was called Koryo or Silla, green leaf tea was the main beverage, but as time went by the cultivation of tea declined while the popularity shifted to herbal and fruit drinks. Introduced below are the names of teas and drinks served in each season.

Winter: Ginger tea, KUGEE-CHA (Chinese matrimony vine tea), YUJA drink, ginseng tea

Summer: TUKYEONHWA fruit drink, iced ginseng tea, mixed fruit juice

The multiformity of Korean cookery can be told by the way they serve desserts. They enjoy numerous kinds of sweets on festive occasions.

Sweet desserts can be classified by the cooking method:
FRIED/YU-GWA: deep-fried cereals
STEWED/JEON-GWA: root (rootcrops) or fruits stewed in honey or sugar syrup
CANDIED/TA-GWA: honey-nut nougat
STEAMED/TA-SIK: steamed rice and nuts in sesame oil and honey

Another tradition on festivals or events are steamed rice cakes. They are eaten in various forms: "White Snow" rice cake on birthdays, New Year's rice cake in soup, herbal rice cake to welcome the spring, square rice cakes on Children's day in May, cinnamon rice cake on Star Festival in July, pine rice cakes on moon-viewing evenings, radish or chrysanthemum flower rice cake on chrysanthemum-appreciating day in autumn, rice dumplings to charm away a plague in winter, etc., etc.

BAMBOO MAT

Narrow strips of bamboo are held together by cotton strings. Bamboo mat is used for shaping soft ingredients and to make rolled rice such as ROLLED RICE WITH *NORI* SEAWEED (P 70).

HOW TO USE BAMBOO MAT

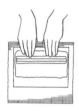

① Place *nori* seaweed on bamboo mat then the rice and fillings as illustrated. Lift front end of the bamboo mat with thumbs. Press rice slightly with rest of fingers.

② Roll everything together in the direction of the far end of the bamboo mat. Press Slightly.

③ Adjust the form of the rolled rice by squeezing it gently and carefully.

BAMBOO STEAMERS

For effective steaming, put on a wok filled with boiling water. Bamboo steamers can steam any ingredients and can be stacked in two or three layers to steam different foods at a time. Good things about bamboo steamers are that the mesh lid controls the steam and does not drip onto ingredients. Choose 12 in (30cm) diam steamer for a regular wok.

COOKING SCISSORS

Convenient for cutting off fish fins or chicken wings, and for cutting hard ingredients such as bean threads. Usually have other functions like opening bottlecaps or cracking nuts.

COPPER POT

Conducts heat quickly, therefore a good pot for table cooking. Polish once a month since the copper can easily tarnish and may be poisonous. Use mixture of lemon juice and salt for best copper polish and burnish.

EARTHEN POT OR CASSEROLE

Good for table cooking. Once it is heated through, it maintains the heat. If using a new earthen pot, do as follows: Fill with heavily salted hot water. Heat until the water decreases. Allow to cool. Pour in hot water again and heat to boiling. This will make the pot durable for long time use.

If the bottom is burnt, do not scrub but pour in vinegar and water; heat 10 minutes and then scrub. Do not scour outer bottom.

COOKING UTENSILS

MEASURING UTENSILS

Measuring by the eye often causes waste of food or failure of seasoning. Be sure to measure in the right way.

Kitchen Scales
For home use, choose 5 lb/2 kg scales, with a large dish. Flat plate does not hold flour or nuts well. Do not leave things on the dish as it damages the spring.

Measuring Cup
1 cup is equivalent to 240 ml in this book. Usually made of glass, stainless or plastic. Stainless cups are most durable while glass ones are easy to read.

Measuring Spoons
There are four graduated sizes, tablespoon (T), teaspoon (t), half teaspoon (½ t), and quarter teaspoon (¼ t). 1 tablespoon is equivalent to 15 ml or 3 teaspoons. 1 teaspoon equals 5 ml. To measure dry ingredients, scoop into appropriate spoon until full, and level with a spatula/knife.

METAL STRAINER

Ideal for straining dry and liquid ingredients and also useful for sifting small amount of dry ingredients.

MICROWAVE RANGE

For cooking foods speedily and cleanly. Without heating the utensils or oven, only the foods are heated. The food must contain moisture, and metal container or china with metal decorations are not suitable (metals cause sparks). Microwaves do a good job in thawing frozen meats or fish.

PRESSURE COOKER

For quick cooking. Cooking by superheated steam under pressure reduces cooking time to ¼–⅕ of what conventional pan takes. Ideal for BRAISED SHORT RIBS WITH VEGETABLES (P 28) or OXTAIL SOUP (P 14).

SQUARE OMELET PAN

Square omelet pan is used in Oriental cooking to make various omelets, from paper-thin to steak-thick, and also rolled omelets. Choose small sized, oblong pan for home use.

WOK

A wok has many advantages for deep-frying, stir-frying, sautéeing and steaming. Because of its large surface area which keeps food moving quickly, the rounded bottom requires a minimum amount of oil, and the slanted sides protects against splattering. To give the wok stability, place the adapter ring over the largest burner, with the sides slanting upwards to allow the center of the wok in closer proximity to the burner.

A newly purchased wok should be given special seasoning. First fill wok ¾ full with water; heat until lukewarm. Add detergent and scrub well with a brush. Repeat. Cut-up half an onion into slices. Heat 2 t oil in the wok until hot over high heat. Add onion slices and stir-fry rotating wok constantly to coat sloping sides with oily slices almost burnt black. Discard the onion and oil. Wash the wok with hot water and dry.

Whenever the wok is used for steaming, it must be reseasoned afterward in order to prevent food from sticking. The cover and steaming rack are for steaming food. A steaming rack, made of metal is used to elevate plates of food above the boiling water in wok whilst steaming.

INGREDIENTS

CHRYSANTHEMUM LEAVES

The perfume and blossoms of this vegetable are like chrysanthemums bred for garden display and cutting. But the edible foliage of the ''spring'' or ''leaf'' chrysanthemum are more deeply lobed and fuller than the decorative variety. The best ones are sold with roots attached. If you cannot obtain it, watercress or young spinach can be used as substitutes.

DAIKON RADISH

Daikon radish is otherwise known as icicle radish. It is rich in vitamins, and its leaves contain a lot of calcium. This radish is thought to aid in digesting oily foods. It is good for simmered dishes.

ENOKITAKE MUSHROOMS

Enokitake mushrooms are mild-flavored and have a pleasant crispness and aroma. They are often used in soups. They are canned *enokitake* mushrooms but fresh ones are better.

GARLIC

Garlic is the pungent and strong-scented bulb of a European herb from the lily family. Korean cooking is not ethnic without this flavor. The stalks are also edible and can be used in stir-fried dishes.

Rich in glucide and vitamin B_1, garlic has a substance called arithin which unites with vitamin B_1 and prevents vitamin B_1 from destruction.

Although garlic is thought to be a food for stamina, it activates circulations and also stimulates the secretion of gastric juice. Therefore it is thought to be effective on colds, insomnia, parasites, neuralgia, muscular pains, and preventive for hardening of the arteries and high blood pressure.

Besides this it is said to work as a tranquilizer. Because of its strong effect on the body, overeating damages stomach and liver. Take a little amount regularly. Whole garlic marinated in soy sauce (See P 85–GARLIC PICKLES) has less odor and is easy to eat.

GINGER ROOT

Ginger is a pungent, aromatic rootstalk of a genus Zingiber, tropical Asiatic and Polynesian herb. It is a popular spice all over the world. It has no specific minerals, but makes a popular condiment in Korean cookery.

The pungent substance promotes both appetite and digestion.

When using for stir-fried dishes, shred and cook in hot oil to extract the aroma. In this oil cook the other ingredients. Choose fresh root without wrinkles.

INGREDIENTS

GREEN ONION

Green onion has been a contribution to Korean cookery as well as garlic has. The green onion referred to in this book is not the same as the green onion commonly found in U.S. markets. Substitutes are "leek", "scallion" and sometimes even "shallot".

HOT GREEN PEPPER

Hot green pepper is unripe hot red pepper. The color and shape resemble small green pepper, but the hotness resembles the hot red pepper.

It is pickled in salt or KOCHU JANG (hot sauce–See P 95) and eaten all the year round. It is also used to season COLD KIMCHEE DRINKS (See P 83) and as a condiment for soups or one-pot dishes.

HOT RED PEPPER/CHILI PEPPER

Hot red pepper or chili pepper is a member of genus Capsicum. Ripe pepper pods are used as a spice to give a hot and pungent flavor. Sold in fresh and dried forms. Dried hot pepper is sliced or ground. There are three types of ground pepper; flaked, medium, and powdered.

Flaked hot pepper contains seeds and is very hot, but gives vivid color. Medium-ground hot pepper is recommendable for recipes in this book, whereas KOCHU JANG (hot sauce–See P 95) is made from powdered hot pepper. Shredded hot red pepper is used to garnish dishes.

① Powdered chili pepper (chili powder)
② Medium-ground chili pepper
③ Flaked chili pepper
④ Shredded chili pepper
⑤ Whole chili pepper

KOREAN NOODLES

Korean noodles are made mainly from buckwheat. Flour or potato starch is added to give smoothness. There are slight differences of ingredients according to the region. There are also many shapes and sizes just like spaghetti.

When cooked, they turn translucent and smooth textured, yet are very soft on the tongue. Cooked noodles must be transferred into cold water immediately using a colander. Rince well using fingertips to remove sliminess. This process gives the noodles a specially smooth texture.

The soup for Korean noodles is made from beef, chicken, or pheasant, and chilled well. Add KIMCHEE liquid to this tasty cold soup, if desired.

MIRIN

Mirin is heavily sweetened *sake*, used for cooking. *Mirin* is called "sweet cooking rice wine." *Sake* sweetened with sugar can be a substitute.

MISO

Miso is fermented soybean paste. The colors range from yellow to brown; yellow *miso* is referred to as white *miso* in this book and brown *miso* as red *miso*. It might be helpful to learn about *miso* by buying small quantities of various kinds. It is used for soups, dressings, sauces, etc.

INGREDIENTS

NORI SEAWEED

The best quality *nori* seaweed is a glossy black-purple. It is used after toasting which improves flavor and texture. *Nori* seaweed grows around bamboo stakes placed under water. When the time comes, it is gathered, washed, laid in thin sheets and dried. It contains lots of iodine.

SESAME OIL

Sesame oil is said to be most aromatic of all oils. It works as well as the seeds. It is notable that because of the abundant vitamin E, it oxidizes very slowly, therefore it keeps well.

Sesame oil may sound Chinese, but it is an essential oil in Korean cookery. Used in various ways such as stir-fried food, barbecue, and salad dressings. Sprinkling over the food just before serving adds a good flavor and shine.

PINE NUTS

Pine nuts have been called "Wizard's Elixir" since early times in Korea. Korean white pine bears large cones consisting of nutritious nuts. They are a good source of protein, lipids, vitamin B_1, B_2, C, calcium and phosphor. They have the most lipid of all nuts. These substances work to improve the internal organs. They are effective on high blood pressure, reumatism, neuralgia, colds, asthma, gout, etc.

Raw or roasted pine nuts are eaten as a snack, and crushed nuts are a good garnish for gruel rices.

SESAME SEEDS

Sesame seeds are divided into three types; white, balck, and yellow. Rich in lipids, white seeds are used to make sesame oil while strong-scented black seeds are used as a seasoning for rice or cakes. Aromatic yellow seeds are not produced enough for home use.

Lipids occupy more than half content of sesame seeds, and are effective on preventing cholesterol from settling down. Therefore it is said to be a good food for preventing hardening of the arteries. Also protein makes up nearly 20% of the rest of the content. Calcium, iron, vitamin B_1, B_2, nicotinic acid are also good for preventing anemia and constipation.

Eaten in toasted or ground forms.

SALTED OPOSSUM SHRIMP

Opossum shrimp is $3/8$ in (1 cm) long, shrimp-like arthropod. It is salted and used as an essential ingredient of KIMCHEE. When added to the salted vegetables in fermenting process, it produces, vitamin B_{12} and at the same time amino acid.

It is also eaten with white rice. It adds a rich flavor to any dish, together with its liquid.

INGREDIENTS

SHIITAKE MUSHROOMS

Both fresh and dried *shiitake* mushrooms can be obtained. Dried ones should be soaked in water before using. This soaking water makes *dashi* stock. Fresh *shiitake* mushrooms have a distinctive, appealing "woody-fruity" flavor. *Shiitake* mushrooms are good for simmered dishes because of their special flavor. The best ones have thick, brown velvety caps and firm flesh.

SHIMEJI MUSHROOMS

Fresh *shimeji* mushrooms should be delicate-crisp, and like *enokitake* mushroom in texture. The stems should be short and plump, and the flesh should be white. White mushrooms will do as a substitute if *shimeji* is not available.

SOYBEAN SPROUTS

Soybean sprouts are artificially grown in the shade. With softened soybeans still attached, they are rich in protein and minerals, specially in vitamin B_1, B_2 and C. They retain the good flavor and texture even when added to the rice to steam with.

Boiled and seasoned soybean sprouts (See P 44 – ASSORTED VEGETABLES) is a typical Korean salad and also a must in BIBIMBAP (VEGETABLES AND BEEF ON RICE–See P 64).

Choose those which have plump beans and pale yellow stems. Remove roots for a better texture. When parboiling, start with water and cover. Do not remove the lid until the water boils, otherwise a greasy smell will remain.

SOY SAUCE

Soy sauce is made from soy beans and salt. It is the primary seasoning in Korean cooking. It is used for simmered foods, dressings, soups– many kinds of Korean dishes. There are two kinds of soy sauce. One is ordinary soy sauce and the other is light soy sauce, which has a paler color and is less salty and does not darken the color of the foods. Soy sauce gives a delicate flavor and taste to foods.

TOFU

Usually square shaped, creamy textured, bland curd made from soybeans. Also comes deep-fried or canned. Fresh *tofu*, covered with water, can be kept in the refrigerator for approximately one week. Remove from original package and replace with fresh water as soon as possible. Change water every 2 days to keep fresh. *Tofu* is rich in proteins, vitamins, and minerals. It is low in calories and saturated fats, and entirely free of cholesterol.

WAKAME SEAWEED

This seaweed is usually sold in dried form. *Wakame* seaweed can be used for various soups. It is also a good salad ingredient. It should not be simmered for more than a minute. *Wakame* seaweed is rich in vitamins and proteins.

METRIC TABLES

Today many areas of the world use the metric system and more will follow in the future. The following conversion tables are intented as a guide to help you.

General points of information that may prove valuable or of interest:
1 British fluid ounce = 28.5 ml
1 American fluid ounce = 29.5 ml

1 Japanese cup = 200 ml
1 British cup = 200 ml = 7 British fl oz
1 American cup = 240 ml = 8 American fl oz

1 British pint = 570 ml = 20 British fl oz
1 American pint = 470 ml = 16 American fl oz
T = tablespoon oz = ounce g = gram ml = milliliter

Weights

ounces to grams*	grams to ounces
1/4 oz = 7 g	1 g = 0.035 oz
1/2 oz = 14 g	5 g = 1/6 oz
1 oz = 30 g	10 g = 1/3 oz
2 oz = 60 g	28 g ≑ 1 oz
4 oz = 115 g	100 g = 3 1/2 oz
6 oz = 170 g	200 g = 7 oz
8 oz = 225 g	500 g = 18 oz
16 oz = 450 g	1000 g = 35 oz

grams × 0.035 = ounces
ounces × 28.35 = grams

* Equivalent

Linear Measures

inches to centimeters	centimeters to inches*
1/2 in = 1.27 cm	1 cm = 3/8 in
1 in = 2.54 cm	2 cm = 3/4 in
2 in = 5.08 cm	3 cm = 1 1/8 in
4 in = 10.16 cm	4 cm = 1 1/2 in
5 in = 12.7 cm	5 cm = 2 in
10 in = 25.4 cm	10 cm = 4 in
15 in = 38.1 cm	15 cm = 5 3/4 in
20 in = 50.8 cm	20 cm = 8 in

inches × 2.54 = centimeters
centimeters × 0.39 = inches

in = inch   cm = centimeter

Temperatures

Fahrenheit (F) to Celsius (C)		Celsius (C) to Fahrenheit (F)	
freezer storage	−10°F = −23.3°C	freezer storage	−20°C = −4°F
	0°F = −17.7°C		−10°C = 14°F
water freezes	32°F = 0 °C	water freezes	0°C = 32°F
	68°F = 20 °C		10°C = 50°F
	100°F = 37.7°C		50°C = 122°F
water boils	212°F = 100 °C	water boils	100°C = 212°F
	300°F = 148.8°C		150°C = 302°F
	400°F = 204.4°C		200°C = 392°F

The water boiling temperature given is at sea level.

Conversion factors:

$$C = \frac{(F - 32) \times 5}{9}$$

$$F = \frac{C \times 9}{5} + 32$$

C = Celsius   F = Fahrenheit

INDEX

A
appetizers   10–13
ASSORTED VEGETABLES   44
automatic rice cooker   93

B
BAKED SPARERIBS   22
bamboo mat   104
bamboo steamers   104
BARBECUED MEAT   20
Barbecue Sauces (soy sauce, miso)   21
BEEF AND VEGETABLE HOT POT   26
beef stock   94
BIBIMBAP   64, 99, 102
boiled egg   12
BOILED POTATOES AND BEEF   52
BOUILLABAISSE–KOREAN STYLE   34
BRAISED SHORT RIBS WITH VEGETABLES   28
BRAISED TOFU   61
BROILED FISH   39
BUPJU   9, 103

C
casserole   104
CHICKEN SOUP   18
chicken stock   94
chili pepper   90, 107
chili pepper, shredded   107
chili powder   95, 107
CHINESE CABBAGE KIMCHEE   80
Chinese matrimony vine tea   9, 103
chrysanthemum leaves   106
CLAM BAKE   40
CLAMS AND WAKAME SEAWEED   42
COLD CUCUMBER SOUP   19
COLD KIMCHEE DRINKS   83
COLD NOODLE DISH   72
COLD NOODLES WITH HOT SAUCE   75
cooked rice   92
COOKED RICE IN HOT BROTH   65
COOKED RICE IN OXTAIL SOUP   15
cooking scissors   104
copper pot   104
COUNTRY STYLE BEEF   12

D
daikon radish   106
DAIKON RADISH KIMCHEE   82
DAIKON RADISH PICKLES   84
DAIKON RADISH WITH CHICKEN   53
dashi-no-moto (instant stock)   94
dashi stock   94
dried sardines   94

E
earthen pot or casserole   104
egg batter coated food   56, 57, 98
eggs   56–59
enokitake mushrooms   106

F
fiddlehead   44
firm tofu   56, 60, 61, 62
FISH SOUP   17
FRESH FISH WITH HOT SAUCE   32

G
garlic   85, 90, 106
GARLIC PICKLES   85
ginger root   106
ginseng   9, 103
green onion   107
grilled food   98
ground chili pepper   107
GRUEL RICE WITH CHICKEN   67
GRUEL RICE WITH VEGETABLES   66

H
hot green pepper   107
HOT GREEN PEPPERS IN MISO PASTE   87
HOT NOODLE DISH   74
hot red pepper   107
HOT–SPICY FISH STEW   36

K
KEBAB KOREAN STYLE   57
KIMCHEE   80–83, 99
kitchen scales   105
KOCHU JANG (hot sauce)   95
Korean noodles   72–75, 107
KUGEE–CHA   9, 103
KUJEOLPAN   4, 78
KUKBAP   15, 65, 99

L
LEAF ROLLS   11

M
matsutake mushrooms   9
McKOLRY   95, 103
measuring cup   105
measuring spoons   105
meats   20–31
meat/seafood au naturel   25, 32, 96
metal strainer   105
microwave range   105
MILSAM   78
mirin   107
miso   107
MIXED VEGETABLES WITH BEEF   46
MIXED VEGETABLES WITH SEAFOOD   47

N
NAMOOL   44
noodles   72–79, 99
nori seaweed   13, 58, 70, 108

O
one-pot dishes   96
OVEN-BARBECUED SPARERIBS   23
oxtails   14, 15, 23
OXTAIL SOUP   14

P
pear   25, 72,
pickles   80–87, 99
pine nuts   108
PORK AND KIMCHEE CASSEROLE   31
preserves   88
pressure cooker   105

R

red leaf lettuce 11
red-purple seaweed 43
rice 64–71, 92, 99
RICE WITH SOYBEAN SPROUTS 68
ROLLED–EGG–OMELET 58
ROLLED HAM 10
ROLLED RICE WITH NORI SEAWEED 70

S

salads 97
SALTED CLAMS 88
salted opposum shrimp 59, 80, 82, 108
SALTED OYSTERS 88
SAM JANG 11
SAUTÉED MUSHROOMS 48
seafoods 32–43
SEAFOOD AND VEGETABLE OMELET 56
SEAFOOD SALAD 43
SEASONED RAW BEEF 25
SENGCHE 11, 44, 97
sesame oil 90, 108
sesame seeds 108
shiitake mushrooms 109
shimeji mushrooms 48, 109
shiso leaves 86
SHISO LEAVES IN MISO PASTE 86
shredded omelet 41, 94
SHRIMP AND VEGETABLE WRAP–UPS 78
simmered food 97
SINSEON–LO 4, 96
SKEWERED BEEF AND VEGETABLES 24
small green pepper 51
soups 14–19, 96
soybean sprouts 44, 64, 68, 69, 109
soy sauce 109
SPICY STIR–FRIED SQUID 37
square omelet pan 41, 58, 71, 105
STEAMED BUNS 76
STEAMED CLAMS 41
STEAMED EGG CUSTARD 59
STEAMED FISH 38
steamed food 98
STEAMED SMALL GREEN PEPPERS 51
STEAMED TONGUE 29
STIR–FRIED CUCUMBERS AND BEEF 50
stir-fried food 97
STIR–FRIED GARLIC STALKS 49
STIR–FRIED PORK WITH KIMCHEE 30
STIR–FRIED RICE 69
STUFFED CABBAGE ROLLS 54
SUKCHE 11, 44, 97
sushi rice 70

T

tendons 94
TOASTED NORI SEAWEED 13
tofu 54, 56, 60–63, 109
TOFU CASSEROLE WITH MISO 63
TOFU HOT POT 62
TOFU STEAK 60

V

vegetables 44–55
VEGETABLES AND BEEF ON RICE 64
VEGETABLE SOUP 16

W

wakame seaweed 18, 19, 42, 109
WHITE FISH SALAD 33
WOK 105

Y

YAKBAP 99
YANG NYEOM JANG 95